Once Upon a Sandbox

Once Upon a Sandbox

C. R. Wilker

To my dear friend, Judy, who has been been with this project, every step of the way,

Carolyn Wilker
June 23, 2011

Reflections on the Past

First Edition

A division of
www.HiddenBrookPress.com
writers@HiddenBrookPress.com

Copyright © 2011 Hidden Brook Press
Copyright © 2011 C. R. Wilker

All rights for story and characters revert to the author. All rights for book, layout and design remain with Hidden Brook Press. No part of this book may be reproduced except by a reviewer who may quote brief passages in a review. The use of any part of this publication reproduced, transmitted in any form or by any means, electronic, mechanical, photocopied, recorded or otherwise stored in a retrieval system without prior written consent of the publisher is an infringement of the copyright law.

Once Upon a Sandbox
by C. R. Wilker

Cover Art – Deborah Pryce
Cover Design – Richard M. Grove
Layout and Design – Richard M. Grove

Typeset in Garamond
Printed and bound in USA

Library and Archives Canada Cataloguing in Publication

Wilker, C. R. (Carolyn R.), 1950-
    Once upon a sandbox / C.R. Wilker. -- 1st ed.

ISBN 978-1-897475-69-0

    1. Wilker, C. R. (Carolyn R.), 1950- --Childhood and youth. 2. Wilker, C. R. (Carolyn R.), 1950- --Family. 3. Farm life--Ontario. I. Title.

S522.C3W55 2011   C818'.609   C2011-903498-0

*Dedicated to my parents,
who know what it takes
to make a home.*

Acknowledgements

Thank you to my parents, siblings and members of my extended family for permission to share their stories in my book. Thank you to my husband who made meals while I wrote and edited and also to my daughters and partners for their encouragement in the writing process. I wish I could thank Aunt Doris for her enthusiasm when I was beginning to write and get published. To name her here will have to do.

Thank you to early teachers of reading and writing, in that one-room schoolhouse and beyond, and to family or friends at a distance who expressed their appreciation for my long letters or travelogues, an early expression of the writer-to-be.

Thanks also to editors who guided my early submissions and for those friends and fellow writers whose enthusiasm has buoyed me on the journey. You know who you are.

Thank you to Kathleen Bickle for sharing valuable material about the Women's Institutes, and the beginning of the 4-H club as I knew it, and for time to ask questions and listen to her experiences as a member of the organization. Thanks to Mary Lou Ross, who helped me to recall Achievement Day memories and brought me up to date on the changes in 4-H clubs.

My appreciation to fellow Toastmasters and storytellers who listened to my stories and to Sally Russell whose book, *Latitudes of Home*, challenged and inspired me to unlock my own memories, including some stories tucked away in computer files, waiting for a home. Thank you to members of Muses Ink, my first critique group; and to members of The Word Guild, a helpful and encouraging group of writers and editors. Thank you to fellow Revision members for helping me to shape the prose and poetry that I shared in that forum.

Thank you to my fellow Muse and editor, Susan Deefholts, for helping me to develop my manuscript further and for her enthusiasm for my topic. You've helped me make it so much stronger.

And last but not least, thanks to God for the gift.

"There have been great societies that did not use the wheel, but there have been no societies that did not tell stories."

Ursula K. LeGuin

Table of Contents

ACKNOWLEDGEMENTS – *p. viii*

INTRODUCTION – *p. xvi*

THE LIFE STORY OF A FAMILY FARM – *p. 1*

PART I: MEET THE FAMILY
- MY MOTHER – *p. 10*
- DAD – *p. 17*
- SISTERS – *p. 23*
- OH BROTHER! – *p. 35*
- MY GRANDPARENTS – *p. 41*

PART II: FARM LIFE
- RISKS OF FARMING – *p. 54*
- DARE TO RIDE – *p. 55*
- FARM PETS – *p. 57*
- ENTERTAINMENT – *p. 59*
- ERRANDS WITH DAD – *p. 68*
- PUMP STORIES – *p. 69*
- WHITEWASHING THE BARN – *p. 70*
- DAD'S HIRED HAND – *p. 72*
- FROM THE TRACTOR SEAT – *p. 76*
- GRAIN HARVEST – *p. 77*
- FROZEN WEEDS WERE GOALPOSTS – *p. 78*
- THE TAVISTOCK AGRICULTURAL SOCIETY AND THE FALL FAIR – *p. 79*
- FEDERATED WOMEN'S INSTITUTES AND 4-H GIRLS' CLUBS – *p. 84*

PART II: GROWING UP
Bush Walk – *p. 104*
Trip to the Woodlot – *p. 105*
Sunday Mornings – *p. 108*
Sunday Drives – *p. 109*
A nickel to spend – *p. 110*
Once Upon a Sandbox – *p. 111*
Attic Playhouse – *p. 112*
Pencils, Lunchboxes and Compositions – *p. 113*
Dream Pages – *p. 116*
School Days – *p. 118*
The Music Lesson – *p. 120*
My Amish Friends – *p. 121*
Good Cooks – *p. 126*
Experiments in the Kitchen – *p. 127*
Perfect Pie Crust – *p. 129*
The Garden Club – *p. 130*
Green Hands and Baskets Full of Cucumbers – *p. 133*
What a Car! – *p. 137*

PART III: THE WIDER CIRCLE
　Sam – *p. 144*
　Just like Daddy – *p. 147*
　Anticipated Visits – *p. 148*
　Eggs Away – *p. 150*
　Kitchen Talk – *p. 152*
　Crochet Lessons – *p. 153*
　The Granny Square – *p. 154*
　Persistent Little Sister – *p. 157*
　Sidekicks – *p. 158*
　His Own Way – *p. 161*
　Bringing the Cows Home – *p. 164*
　Memory of a Life – *p. 165*
　From a Cocoon – *p. 169*
　One Last Moonlight – *p. 170*
　February Grief – *p. 172*
　Goodbye to the Old Farm House – *p. 173*

CONCLUSION – *p. 175*

WRITING YOUR OWN STORIES – *p. 179*
ABOUT THE AUTHOR – *p. 180*
PREVIOUSLY PUBLISHED PIECES – *p. 181*
BIBLIOGRAPHY – *p. 182*

Introduction

Every day after lunch, my eighth grade teacher read to our class. We sat at our desks and let our imaginations soar. What a gift he gave us, with tales from *Swiss Family Robinson, Tom Sawyer* and other books.

Johann Wyss and Mark Twain knew how to tell a story. They developed a plot, invented believable characters, and created a setting in which the readers could get immersed. Libraries are full of such books.

In those library shelves are books of many different genres, each with the writers' distinctive styles. We cannot stop there. Consider the revival of the storytelling tradition, families sitting around the table or the fireplace sharing stories. All it takes is for someone to say, "Tell me about my grandfather," and the anecdotes begin.

In 2009, I had a part in gathering my parents' stories for a family history. I learned things about my grandparents and my parents that I didn't know before. Those stories are written from their perspective, and as we know, each person's view of an event will be somewhat different.

In the process of sharing our cultural and familial stories, we can learn much from our native peoples, who share their history largely in the oral tradition. Few of their stories were recorded in written form, but instead were passed down from one generation to the next by spoken word.

I believe that everyone has stories to tell, even if few share them. Stories come from our experiences, in the history that we make each day. They tell us who we are and what influences we've had. Storyteller Dan Yashinsky says in his book, *Suddenly They Heard Footsteps*, that he's connected to his ancestors by the stories his grandmother shared. "Stories were almost all she brought over from Europe." He says that even if some of those stories are hard to listen to, they must be told. He feels obligated to carry those stories forward to the next generation.

Much as Dan feels like the torchbearer, I, too, bring my stories for a new generation to hear, for those who have not known the grandparents in my life and the way things were when I was growing up.

My stories come to you in narrative pieces, in poetry and in prose, specifically creative non-fiction.

Creative non-fiction is different from historical telling and separate from fiction. Stories relayed in this style come from the eyes, the heart, and the viewpoint of the teller. Someone else's version can and will be different, since we are all unique.

I hope this collection will encourage you to share your stories in whatever way is in you to tell. Enjoy.

The Life Story of a Family Farm

This is the story of a family living on a farm that once belonged to my grandparents. It is about the individuals, the personalities and the ties that bind us to each other, in love and in faith, within a community of extended family, neighbours and friends. It is about the challenges and routines of farm life in rural Ontario of the 50s and 60s.

Sustained by their faith, my parents have always looked to the future with optimism, and with the belief that God would provide. These beliefs have buoyed them through both good and uncertain times. My sisters and I have followed that path, even if our careers and families have taken us in different directions. My brother's story is interwoven with ours, starting with the summer when he joined our family.

Despite the demands of life and of the everyday bustle of modern living, it is also important to take the time to remember how we got here and where we came from. To set this dream aside in favour of everyday matters, amid the flow of life, work, seasons, and generations, means the memories would be lost forever. And though the whole story stretches back and back through the centuries, I will begin this book with the story of our family farm.

My grandfather—a city boy—married a country girl who had moved to the city. An old photograph, faded with age, reveals a twenty-four-year-old man wearing a high-collared white shirt with a boutonniere on his dark suit, and a young woman, the same age, wearing a fitted long white dress, with a veil and decorated headpiece. She holds a bouquet of mixed flowers. This was who my grandfather Ted and grandmother Flora were before they became parents to my father and grandparents to me.

In 1915, my grandfather left his job at the head office of the Canadian National Railroad when they bought a farm. They paid $4100 for the house, barn, and 100 acres, which included a five-acre bush lot at the back of the farm. It was a lot of money to pay at that time. To compare it with today's farm prices would be difficult, since farm methods, equipment, and upgrades in buildings have changed so much in the past ninety-four years.

On moving to the farm, my grandmother was returning to the same county, a country block from where she grew up, only now she was coming with a husband, and expecting their first child.

The house, covered with battenboard, had no electricity, and the family depended on kerosene lamps for light and a wood stove for cooking and heat. According to Dad's sister, Aunt Edith, Grandma used paint and pretty wallpaper "to make the old house cozy and nice."

The barn, constructed with hand-hewn beams and mortise and tenon joints, was faced with hemlock boards on the outside. The barn was large enough to shelter horses, cattle, pigs and chickens, with a stable on ground level, and the threshing floor above it. The upper floor, accessed by the sloping hill on one side, also held grain bins and a haymow. A root cellar, which consisted of a separate storage area on the upper level, was used to store root vegetables like turnips or potatoes. Later, when my grandfather decided to increase the chicken operations, he had a two-storey hen house added to one end of the barn.

Looking for a way to make planting and harvesting more efficient, my grandfather bought an 8-16 International chain-driven tractor for $36. Until that time, my grandfather used the work horses to pull the plough and work the fields for planting. According to my father, Ted was much more comfortable driving the team of horses, and so he left driving the tractor to his sons. After he bought the tractor, the horses were used for pulling the sleigh and ploughing Flora's large garden.

#

Dad was born in the farm house, the youngest of my grandparents' five children. He learned to walk, talk, ride a bike, and he helped with chores and spent time with his siblings. As he grew up, he made time for baseball, hockey, and activities with the Junior Farmers organization, while learning about farming. When his older brother bought a farm, my father knew that someday he would have his own farm too.

My grandfather built a new red brick home in 1939, and then tore down the old one. The family moved from one house to another without changing their address. When my parents were married in 1949, they lived with my grandparents for two of those early years.

My parents bought the home farm in 1952, the same year they purchased the 50 acres across the concession road. My grandparents moved to a new home in Stratford.

#

Like my father, I grew up there, played in the yard, rode my bicycle, learned to garden, drove the tractor, pulled mustard from grain fields, picked up stones, podded peas, and walked to the one-room red-brick schoolhouse a quarter mile up the road—the same school my father attended.

There have been many changes in the farm landscape over this time. A bachelor neighbour, named Sam, lived on a lot at the corner of our farm field, but he died late in 1955. Mom and Dad bought his few acres, took down his house and woodshed, and cleared the land around it.

In 1956, Dad built a garage onto the house. A few years later, he constructed a drive shed across the lane from the house, so there would be a place to store implements and to fix tractors and equipment in inclement and winter weather. In 1963, we built a new chicken barn for cage-laying hens. We three older girls helped build those cages, under Dad's watchful eye, using couplers and pliers to put the sections together. We also helped to install those 4300 squawking chickens into their new home.

Instead of painting the barn, which was an expensive undertaking, Dad used whitewash, a mixture of lime and water, to coat the boards and preserve the wood. Mom says we did it every year, though I only remember doing it one summer.

A tornado in 1979 roared over the community, pulled up mature trees and twisted branches off others. It broke hydro lines like they were toothpicks, destroyed homes and barns, and jumped concessions before it descended upon my parents' property. The tornado levelled the top storey of the barn, and brushed by the house, giving it a mighty shake. It snapped off two mature walnut trees on the lawn then moved on to neighbours' homes and farms.

My parents and younger siblings—I had moved away by then, married and had two young children of my own—rushed to the basement, as pieces of the barn were borne aloft by the winds. They emerged shaken, but thankfully not hurt, after the tornado had passed. The house required extensive repairs to beams and bricks, but compared to others who lost their barns and homes, our family was fortunate. In spite of some injuries and broken bones among neighbours, no one died because of the storm.

My youngest sister says it was something to see the wind carry away a barn door that had taken eight strong men to put up. Just as amazing was the way the community pulled together to help each other out.

Two weeks after the tornado had struck, when the cattle and pigs had been sold, Dad started tearing down the rest of the barn. The insurance company had declared the structure dangerous.

Since then, my parents have added an additional drive shed where the old barn once stood, and in 1986, Dad replaced the old garage with a new one and had a sunroom added to the south side of the house.

#

Early in 2009, the latest chapter in the story of our farm was written, when its ownership changed hands. Two of my cousins, sons of my father's older sister, have purchased the farm. They will manage farm operations from their own homes, allowing my parents to stay in our family home. My parents are pleased that the farm will remain in the family and that they can continue to live in the place they've called "home" for so many years. In the growing season, my parents can still plant and tend a garden and maintain the space around them, while someone else ploughs, plants, and harvests crops from the land.

We've celebrated countless anniversaries and birthdays at our family home, and we're glad we can still do that. To my parents, each of my siblings and their respective families, my husband and children, thank you for making those times of togetherness a blessing.

Part I
Meet the Family

My Mother

Lyla

The Tavistock Fall Fair Dance has long been a significant social gathering for the youth in our community. It holds even more significance in the lives of my parents, Harry and Lyla. It was the place they first met. That dance in 1944 is a time that I suspect they will never forget.

This all happened long before Lyla became a wife and mother. She was a daughter, a sister, a cousin, an employee and a friend, and to understand her life now, it is worth looking back at her life before that momentous evening.

Lyla's faith in God is put to the test

My grandparents regularly took their eight children to Sunday school and church. When the small church closed down, they found another one to attend. As the children were old enough to read, they were expected to do their own reading of lessons from Sunday school and church, to guide them in their daily lives.

At about the age of thirteen, Lyla's faith was put to the test. She had gone regularly to market with her parents each week, rising at 4 am each Saturday. She had made friends with other children whose parents rented stands at market. When there wasn't work to be done, Lyla and a particular girl would go off and window shop at Kresge's. One day they boldly made plans for the next week.

The following Friday evening, however, Lyla's mother told her she would not be going to market the next day. Lyla was devastated and began to cry. She could not go to her father for he would stand by his wife's word. Lyla and her friend had not thought to exchange phone numbers, nor did they know each other's last name, and so getting in touch with the other girl was impossible. After many tears, Lyla decided that praying was the only alternative. So she prayed that God would do his work on her parents and went to sleep with that hope in her heart.

Early the next morning, Lyla's mother awakened her at 3:30 am and said she could go to market as usual, if she wished. Lyla, dazed at the seemingly impossible, rose and dressed quickly. "I knew there really was a God, and he had answered my prayers."

It was the beginning of a strong faith she would hold for many years—and that she continues to hold to this very day.

Education in the school of life

It simply wasn't possible for Lyla to go on to high school, though she would have welcomed the opportunity, for she was a good student. Her learning continued at home. Her mother taught her to cook and bake, and Lyla found that she really enjoyed working in the kitchen.

Lyla, having grown up in a large family and living on a farm, had learned the requisite of doing chores from the time she was a young girl, including her least favourite job of filling the wood box in the kitchen before going to school. However, she learned from her family's work ethic and expectations, absorbing them well enough to earn a job at a fruit stand.

She learned bookkeeping when she worked in a store as a young girl. Undaunted, but perhaps disappointed that she could not go on to high school, Lyla nevertheless used what she knew and continued to learn. At the store, without a cash register to add up the amount of a sale and to determine the amount of change to give a customer, she used her strong math and mental arithmetic skills, so she excelled at her job.

Apparently, a manager from another market stopped in one day when she was running the store by herself. He offered her a job at his store. She had to talk with her parents about it, but she promised to consider the offer. Soon afterwards, she had a new job and a raise in pay. Her parents, having collected all her pay to keep the house going, now allowed her to keep some of this money, and so she bought fabric to sew new skirts and dresses and treated herself to ice cream now and then.

Lyla meets Harry

Excited to be attending her first dance—especially the Fall Fair dance—Lyla was dressed in a pleated plaid skirt and a yellow blouse, bobby socks, and saddle shoes, which were high style at the time. She was under the supervision of her older sisters and brothers, enjoying the music, when she saw a young man walking toward her early in the evening.

Harry, wearing dress pants and a sports shirt, asked her to dance. They danced together for two songs, then Harry asked if he could drive her home. Her older brothers approved, and Harry took her home that evening.

Lyla and Harry dated for a few years and were married in June 1949. They lived with Harry's parents on their home farm until Ted and Flora decided to purchase a home in the city, at which time Harry and Lyla—already the parents of two little girls, Mary and me—bought the home farm as well as a lot across the road.

The place and occasion of Mom and Dad's meeting—the Tavistock Fall Fair—has been so much a part of their lives and ours. And yet, I only learned, in working with Mom and Dad on their family history just how strong was their connection with that yearly event. It obviously carries much emotion too. Mom said there never was another man for her after meeting Harry.

My Mother

My mother has a tender heart for others. It shows in her smile and soft blue eyes and willingness to lend her listening ear to a friend or neighbour.

She offered from her abundance to those who experienced difficulty. When I was growing up, our garden was often such a blessing that even after we had what we needed, there was still more. Anyone experiencing hardship could pick from it to feed a family, at least for a few meals.

It often seemed to me that those endless rows of vegetable plants would never stop producing and that the more we shared, the greater the harvest that was reaped. Much of this generosity came, I believe, from her faith that God would provide for our needs, and out of gratitude for what he had already done.

Mom is creative; it shows in her home, her taste in paint and wallpaper, the arrangement of furniture, her crocheted afghan and matching pillows, and the way she displays things. Her creativity shows in her experimentation with oil painting and in her choice of accessories. It showed too in the pretty dresses she sewed for us when we were small, and the clothing she chooses now for special occasions.

The greenery and flowers around my parents' home and garden show signs of her touch too. In fact, both she and Dad have what some call a green thumb—the ability to care for and nurture plants.

#

Busy as she was, helping Dad with farm work and caring for us, her caretaker role went beyond herself and her family, to embrace a wider sector of the community. My parents have been faithful members of their church, serving on church council and other committees, and making sure we got to Sunday school. All these things have cultivated new friendships, grown leadership skills, and have been a meaningful and fulfilling part of their lives.

In the community, my mother has served as a member of the local Agricultural Society and the Women's Institute. Though she has spent many more years on the Agricultural Society, she was an active member of the Anna P. Lewis Women's Institute for some time and served as its president from 1971 to 1974.

Much later, her focus shifted to an emerging palliative care program that started with a church committee and grew to include a wider community of folks. Mom, along with her fellow volunteers, including her sister Doris, worked with people who were spending their last days at home or in outside care, and who were in need of comfort.

#

Mom delegated chores to us as soon as we were able to help: setting the table for a meal, clearing the table afterwards, washing and drying dishes. She took time to teach us how to do those jobs well. She gave us opportunities to try new tasks and did not scold us when the completed project didn't look as good as hers. We often learned by working alongside her in the kitchen[1] or picking produce in the garden.

As we grew older, we took on more responsibility, as she had when she was growing up. In harvest season especially, when garden produce and fruit from the orchard was ripe and waiting, she did what must have seemed like endless canning and preserving of apples, pears and cherries (when the birds didn't get them) as well as the peas, corn, cucumbers and beets that we grew at home. Mom was also certain to get a bushel or two of peaches that we enjoyed in and out of season. We learned by helping her with those tasks too.

[1] - See "Good Cooks" - *p. 126*

#

Mom is a hard worker and skilled at what she does. She can bake a pie with a perfect flaky crust, a skill her granddaughters now wish to learn from her. She is well organized; she knew on Saturday what we'd wear to church the next day, so that our clothes were ready and our shoes were shined. And she helped Dad run the farm, including handling the book keeping.

It's no wonder that she fell asleep within minutes of putting her head on the pillow at night. This is also the reason why she had read so few books in those years, having fallen asleep before making it to page two. She's more than made up for the lack of reading since then, with a shelf full of interesting books, both fiction and non-fiction.

If there are any regrets, she says, it's that she wishes she had taken more time for fun, and that she had taken us places. Still, we spent a lot of time together, playing games, doing puzzles, going out for ice-cream, taking yearly trips to Ipperwash beach, and talking while we worked together. I've learned so much from my mother—things I'd never learn at high school. I learned how to be disciplined and organized, how to take care of myself and those around me. She taught me much about cooking and baking, and how to can fruits and vegetables. Like her, I sometimes forget to take time to play or just sit and relax. Unlike her, I have cultivated a lifelong habit of reading, regardless of other responsibilities—but then it's been a while since I lived on a farm.

Dad

Being a tender-hearted man, Dad rarely scolded us. He smiled often and his blue eyes rested lovingly on us; I always felt protected and cared for. He has always been strong and agile, sometimes giving us piggyback rides when we were small. I'd hang on around his strong neck and shoulders so I wouldn't fall.

Dad liked to make things for our playtime, and he spent time with us whenever he could. When we were small, he built us a swing set, a teeter totter (which some call a see-saw), and a sandbox, which occupied us through many contented hours of play.

Mom and Dad bought toy tractors, small trucks and cars for playing in the sand. We were allowed to drag the hose to the sandbox and add water to the sand to make mud pies, roads and ponds—water that eventually drained away through the sand to the ground below. We'd kick off our shoes and get right into the gritty warm sand, feeling it and the cool water squishing through our toes. We'd build roads and riverbeds, castles and towers, until we wore sand from head to toe.

Living on a farm meant that we spent a lot of time with both parents. Dad's work was right there on our home land, albeit sometimes in the far extremities of the field. Still, it was close enough that he could come in for meals.

In summer, we had breakfast, lunch and supper with both parents, unless it was a harvest day and Mom and Dad were out working in the field. Then we still got to see them when we took lunch out to them.

Dad gave Mary and me wheelbarrow rides when we were very small, and I'm sure has done that with my other siblings as well. He took us along to the field behind the orchard when he went to feed the chickens. When we were older, we walked there with Dad to close up the coops at night after the chickens were inside roosting. The laying hens were in the barn, but the ones we'd use for eating got to run loose in the field all day.

In the hen house, we put up with flying feathers and lots of dust, but in the coops in the field, the feathers were scattered everywhere, and we had to avoid stepping into smelly chicken poop as much as possible. We'd close the door and latch it, so foxes wouldn't come at night and snatch the chickens. In the morning, we'd have to go and let the chickens out again. Eventually, Mary and I progressed to doing this job ourselves, while Dad worked on other things.

Our father also taught us how to drive tractors, first the Cub Cadet, with attached mower, for mowing the large lawn around our house. Later, when we were old enough, he taught us to drive the Farmall.

Dad is patient, and he has always been careful to work safely himself, so he wanted us to be safe too. He gave plenty of instructions, and when we first tried a new job, he'd stay with us awhile to make sure we could operate the machinery and do the job.

We girls, and later Wayne too, drove the tractor to pull a wagonload of bales on our 100 acres or across the road to the 50 acres we owned there. Before we were old enough to drive on the road, we drove only on the "home farm" as we called it.

Dad warned us about the dangers of the auger and power takeoff when we unloaded grain into the granary, and to be careful of the twisting action inside it, so we wouldn't get our clothing caught on it and hurt ourselves. The power takeoff used energy from the tractor's battery to run another piece of equipment, like the auger, which was an elevator shaft that moved the grain up a closed tube. Dad set one end of the auger into the wagon load of grain and aimed the other end into a window in the second storey of the barn, and the grain would shoot right into the granary. The auger was a time saver; we no longer had to shovel the wheat or barley by hand, but we still had to be careful.

After Dad cut the hay, it had to be raked so it would dry before baling. When the straw or hay were dry, and if there was rain forecasted, we might have to stop some other task to get the baling done before the rain came.

When we were old enough to help with haying and bringing in straw, Mary usually drove the tractor, and I stood on the moving wagon behind the baler, waiting for Dad to grab the bales from the baling machine and hand them to me. I soon learned to stack a load of hay or straw and keep my balance on a moving wagon.

I probably insisted on wearing shorts the first time, since it was so hot, but the cut ends of the hay and straw were sharp and scratched my legs while I handled the bales. The scratches took a while to heal. From then on, I'd hurry into the house and change to summer pants when I knew we'd be haying. I liked working with Dad on the wagon. We were a team, and I worked hard to keep up.

Later, Dad trusted me to try ploughing with the big M tractor, a much bigger and more powerful tractor than the Farmall. Driving tight along the edge of the furrow, where the ground is firm, is almost as tricky as turning on the headland. Too tight a turn at the end of the field and a tractor can tip over. The driver must take as much—or even more—care driving a tractor in the field as he or she would while driving a car on the road.

It takes many hours to plough a field. I'd get off the tractor and feel somewhat shaky after sitting on it a while, going over the bumpy ground. Dad spent many more hours on the tractor. I wonder if he ever felt the same way.

I didn't plough a second time, by choice. I much preferred driving the smaller tractor and harrowing, which involves breaking up the ground further and getting it ready for planting. Backing a wagon into the drive shed was another challenging task. It would always start to jack knife, and I always had to ask Dad to finish that job.

Dad liked tinkering with the tractors and farm equipment and making things work, but the combine often tested his patience, breaking down in the middle of a harvest day. Quite often he could repair it somehow, but sometimes even he had to call it quits and go to Harley's for a part.

Not all about work

Even with all the work on the farm, Dad still made time for fun. Crazy about baseball himself, and having played on a young adult league, he bought us some ball gloves, a bat and a ball, and taught us to catch and hit. When we managed that and had friends over, we played baseball on a diamond he made in the field.

Having played for the Hickson Flyers in his youth, Dad continued to play hockey in winter, on an adult league. Once a week, farm neighbours, whose winter work hours were shorter, gathered at the arena for a game of shinny (after we kids had gone to bed at night). It didn't matter that some men were in their 20s and others were in their 30s, 40s, or 50s, they had a good time on the ice each week and were ready to go back at it the next week.

Being a good skater and enjoying hockey himself, Dad made sure we each had a pair of skates and opportunities to practise skating. Ice skating has never been one of my particular talents, but we had fun together even through the spills and home hockey games.[2]

#

Dad has always loved to drive. On Sunday afternoons, especially in summer, we toured the county or even further. We older girls were sandwiched together in the back seat, with our baby sister up front with Mom and Dad. As a reward for being good passengers, we often stopped at our favourite place for ice cream before heading home.

We could pick our favourite flavour, sometimes a dip cone—vanilla ice cream with chocolate topping—or some other kind of ice cream. Dad had his own two favourites: maple nut or butterscotch.

---

[2] - See "Entertainment" - *p. 59*

We were never allowed to eat the ice cream in the car, however. Mom supervised us at a picnic table outside, and had the washcloth, which Bonnie called the "lawclosh," ready for sticky hands and faces before we got back into the car for the ride home.

Dad liked to swim too, so he enjoyed the trip to Ipperwash every year as much as we did, though he and Uncle Ken spent more time supervising us in the water and playing catch than they did swimming. But going to the lake was a rare treat, so we all enjoyed those days away.

Dad loves music too. He had taken some early guitar lessons when he was a boy, but his steel guitar stood in the back of the closet until Bonnie showed interest in it, preferring it over piano lessons.

Though Dad had little formal musical training, he always enjoyed singing and hearing good music. I often heard him whistle tunes as he worked, and try as I might, have never been able to whistle as easily or as tunefully as he does. He also sang in the church choir for many years, before joining a community choir.

As we worked on the family history together, I learned more about Dad's fascination with trees. As a young boy, he climbed almost every tree on their property. On our yearly trips to the bush lot, he taught us the names of trees and taught us to treat them with care. He had learned how to prune the orchard trees and how to graft a branch from one tree to another, when to spray and when not to do it. He comes closest to climbing trees now when he climbs a ladder or stands on the tractor's loader to pick apples in the orchard. He still makes the springtime trip to the bush lot with his grandchildren and great grandchildren to teach them about trees and living things. He always warned us and probably still reminds those who accompany him to the bush to watch for burdocks.[3]

#

Dad has always been good to us, ensuring we had time for our education and opportunities for fun. Watching out for our safety has also been a prime concern, in addition to learning how to do the tasks that were waiting. He never shirked in his duties as a parent and provider or in caring for farm animals and doing field work, and he expected that we would follow his lead. His sense of fun, making time for us, has meant a lot to me, and I am glad that he has the time for enjoyment now, after so many years of hard work. He still has that twinkle in his eyes that I remember from when I was little and he had some enjoyable activity in mind.

Sisters

I have four sisters: Mary, Bonnie, Joan and Kim, in order of birth age. Although we share the same heritage, as children of the same parents, we are very different from each other.

---

[3] - See "Trip to the Woodlot" - *p. 105*

Mary

Mary is fifteen months younger than I am. Both of us were blonde-haired as children. We have the same blue eyes as our parents, and a curl in our hair like our mother. Somewhere in our preschool years, Mary caught up and grew taller.

For a long time, our mother dressed us alike, in matching dresses, jumpers, blouses and even matching ribbons on our ponytails. Many people couldn't tell us apart if they didn't know us very well. But the similarity ended with our appearances.

As a youngster, Mary was the more adventurous of the two of us. She tried new things without apparent concern for how people would judge her, and she dived into activities with her whole being. When we were told to stay out of the fields in early spring, Mary had to find out just how muddy it could be, had to experience her boots getting stuck in the muck. She insisted that Bonnie and I go with her, and so we all got in trouble together, not only for disobeying our mother and getting stuck in the field, but for losing a boot or two as well.

Mary also climbed trees more easily, with her longer legs. She loved to go barefoot too. In early summer, I watched her pick her way across the yard, over the fresh gravel, never once yowling about the sharpness of stones, but nonetheless making her way like an uneasy stalker, carefully choosing her next step. By summer's end, the soles of her feet were so toughened that she bragged the stones didn't hurt her feet at all. She walked everywhere in bare feet, including wooden surfaces like our teeter totter, and she often got slivers in her feet. She remembers sitting on the kitchen counter on a summer evening after a bath, while Mom, with tweezers in hand, picked out the slivers.

Mary played piano well and usually volunteered to play first when company came to visit. She played scales and octaves more easily than I did. Her hands were just a little bigger and her fingers were longer, so that helped. We played duets for a school talent show, for visitors to our home, and for at least one Women's Institute meeting, when Mom was a member[4]. I remember sitting on a couch at one lady's home, listening to the women's business meeting and waiting for the moment we could play our duet on the piano in that living room.

Mary and I joined the junior choir at church when we were about seven and eight, and on Sundays, we and other members of the choir wore long black gowns with a white billowy surplice over top of it. We paraded through the church, hymn book in hand, singing the opening hymn as we proceeded down the aisle and up some stairs to the balcony, where we sat during the service, like some angel choir without the halos. The senior choir with their all black gowns sat in the next section, looking straight to the front of the church.

Then after confirmation, Mary and I sang with the senior choir, along with our father. These anthems were more challenging, and had four parts. Mary seemed to enjoy singing as much as I did, though I don't remember her singing a lot at home. Maybe she whistled instead.

---

[4] - See "Federated Women's Istitutes and 4-H Girls' Clubs." - *p. 84*

Sharing a room was not easy, for we were so different. Mary liked the window open at night no matter how cold it was outdoors, whereas I liked to snuggle under the covers and keep warm. It was only a ruse, since long before morning, she was under the covers too.

Our parents bought a desk for our bedroom so that we could do homework away from the busy kitchen. What a mistake! Mary read out loud, when all I wanted was quiet. And it seemed like we should each have a separate half of the room, but splitting the desk into two was not an option either. All this made for some very tense homework sessions.

Blood binds us together, even if sparks go off from time to time. We've each developed our own abilities and preferences since those days of childhood, and we have gone along different career paths. Mary went into hairdressing and sales whereas I went into teaching and sewing, then writing and editing.

Still, we did so many things together that we enjoyed, like playing in the orchard in a temporary tree house, making hollyhock dolls, going to 4-H Girls' club and working on our projects together. We played piano duets and walked to the field to bring the cows home for milking, with the dog following at our heels. We went on outings together as teens, and were in each other's wedding parties as maid or matron of honour. Those are the things we remember when differences of opinion or childhood scuffles are behind us.

Bonnie

Bonnie—once the middle child—had the same black hair as Dad, only she has some curl in her hair, whereas Dad's is straight. She has blue eyes like the rest of us. Animal lover extraordinaire, she was the one hugging the cat in a memorable, casual family photograph. She was also the one who had to wear the matching dresses that Mom had made for Mary and me, until she complained one too many times about wearing the same dress to school two days in a row—my outgrown dress one day, and Mary's the next.

Inquisitive about how things work, Bonnie took things apart. One might think she'd be a mechanic, but that didn't turn out to be the case.

I remember an alarm clock in pieces on the floor, gears and springs laying there when she was done her examination. She abandoned the project with absolutely no idea how to put the pieces back together. In fact, Mom said, when Bonnie was quiet, she had to worry about what her daughter was doing.

Bonnie's curiosity reached dangerous levels when she investigated the mercury in the thermometer and checked out the Gillett's Lye, but she survived those encounters and went on to break both collarbones through antics I have no memory of, except to see her arm in a sling. It's a wonder she survived childhood.

Bonnie was a tag-along sister, being a few years younger than me. She joined us on our trips to the bush, the muddy field, the haymow to look for the new litter of kittens, every bit as adventurous as Mary. She was just as eager to explore anything unusual and interesting. Together the three of us caught grasshoppers from the grain field at harvest time and later released them. Bonnie seemed to love all things living and even complained when Dad ended the life of the rooster that used to chase her in the chicken barn.

Bonnie has always had a great love for animals. When she was quite young, she said that she would be a nurse or a veterinarian. She was the one who insisted her cat be in the house, so she could look after it better. When the cat developed hairballs, Bonnie tried to nurse it back to health[5], but the cat died anyway. When that happened, Mom decreed that there would be no more animals in the house.

Bonnie says now, after years in the nursing profession, that she wouldn't have been a good veterinarian. Though she doctors her own pets back to health, she says she could never end an animal's life. Nursing fits her well, as the aim is to preserve life.

Joan

When Mom brought Joan home from the hospital, I worried that the doctors and nurses had mixed up the babies. I was eight years old and didn't know that a baby could be born with dark hair and then lose it all. I guess I expected her to have blonde hair like Mary

[5] - See "Farm Pets" - *p. 57*

and me, even though Bonnie had dark hair. Too young to remember Bonnie's arrival, and not connecting her dark hair with my new baby sister, I was sure Mom and Dad had the wrong one. But Mom was right. The dark hair fell out and beautiful blonde curly hair replaced it. And she had blue eyes just like mine.

Joan was a gentle soul who played well by herself but also happily alongside other children. She could wear white dresses, since she never seemed to get dirty. Following rules never seemed to cause any problems for her, and she seemed content to do small jobs she was asked to do.

Our eight-year difference in ages seems so little now, but at that time, when I was beginning high school, she was starting Grade One, and when I was in college, she was going into Grade Six. After I was married and had my first child, she was going off to college.

At fourteen, Joan was already an accomplished seamstress. For my wedding, she made a dress for herself, and one each for our mother and younger sister, Kim. The styles of those dresses were detailed, and all the dresses were fitted, Mom's in an A-line style, and Kim's with ruffles and a sash. Joan had made her dress from a print and style that suited her slim athletic frame.

Passionate about figure skating, Joan put her whole energy into her practices and performances and passed the fourth figure and senior bronze dance tests in four or five years' time. As Joan passed certain levels, she coached younger students in her patient and kind way. As I was away at college at the time, I rarely got to see her practise or coach, but I looked forward to the skating carnival, when I would see her perform.

She and Matthew, the son of the figure skating coach, tried pairs skating for a short time, and they learned that working together as a team was quite different than skating alone—not a fond memory for her!

The year that the local skating club chose The Wizard of Oz for their carnival theme, Joan was selected to play the role of Dorothy. This meant that she would skate a solo for the song "Follow the Yellow Brick Road."

In the cool of the arena, a community gathered to watch the young people skate, from the toddlers, who made their way around the ice, falling and getting up again, to the more experienced skaters, who made skating look easy. When it was time for Joan's solo, she made her way onto the ice, paused, and waited for her music. In the path of yellow lights that was the yellow brick road to Oz, she skated in such a way that it looked like she was skipping. She twirled, skated backwards, jumped and landed smoothly, skated figure eights, then performed a flying camel and a sit spin to end her three-minute solo.

I was proud of her. I knew that solo, short as it was, took many hours of practice to learn the jumps and spins and do them so well. She put her whole heart into the sport and had excelled. I envied her grace and ease of movement on the ice, but not the time spent in the cold arena for all that practice.

At some point, part-time jobs and school became a priority and skating became a less important activity, although figure skating always held a tender spot in her heart. Joan excelled in her school work and especially loved history and math. She helped on the farm by gathering eggs and driving the tractor for field work. The balance had changed at home with the adoption of Wayne. Joan said, "Certain responsibilities had to be realigned to help support a struggling younger brother and our parents."

Joan attended Westervelt College in London, Ontario, and took business courses, which prepared her well for the work she does today with an accounting firm.

Kim

Kim, thirteen years younger than me, was also fair-haired and blue-eyed. She was the youngest child until soon after her eighth birthday, when Wayne made his appearance. I remember more about her babyhood than any other sister, with the exception of Joan. I was old enough to diaper her, to scoop her up in my arms and dress her, and also to hang out diapers on the clothesline, then to reel the line back in, unclip them from the line, stiff as a board on a cold winter day, only to have them soften again in a warm kitchen as I folded them.

I also had babysitting privileges by that time, meaning that I was left in charge when Mom went to the barn to do chores in an evening. Keeping an eye on a busy preschooler as I tried to do math and history homework at the end of a long school day was both challenging and tiring.

I thought Kim had an enviable place as baby of the family. No longer were Mom and Dad so worried about survival of their children. They were much more relaxed at child rearing, and a good thing too, since Kim was the fifth child and there was much work to do on a farm. Saying "no" was not such a difficult thing to do, and when Mom said it, Kim moved on to her older sisters to try to get what she wanted.

Being five years younger than Joan, just as Joan was five years younger than Bonnie, Kim was the only child at home during the school day, except if Mom was babysitting for a neighbour or family member, and so Kim learned to play by herself. As with most young children, she preferred to bring her toys to play at Mom's feet as Mom cooked and prepared food or did work around the house.

Kim also spent much time playing with our dog and families of cats, which she adored, even to dressing a certain cat and trying to give it a ride in her doll buggy.[6] Such a creative imagination she had and still does.

Kim was eight years old when Wayne arrived at our home, and by that time I was away from home teaching and only around on weekends. I missed a good deal of the adjustment when Kim became a big sister and much of Wayne's early time with our family.

Kim joined the local figure skating club as soon as she was old enough to be enrolled. She enjoyed skating so much that she continued with the club until she was almost 19. Having passed a number of skating and dance tests, and skating in club carnivals, she decided to try out for the precision skating team. She skated on the club team until the beginning of her fourth season.

[6] - See "Farm Pets" - *p. 57*

I was always amazed at the skaters performing as one, and especially at the sequences involved when a small group in the middle skates round and round in a tight circle, while adding new members on each rotation and then performing the same moves in a highly choreographed pattern. I was sure I could never do that, which added all the more to my enjoyment.

As well as skating and her high school studies, Kim took on a part-time job at 15 at the Bonnie Brae nursing home in town, where she worked as a nurse's aide, as I had done earlier. Except for the months that she studied at Sheridan College, she worked at the nursing home until she was married at twenty-five.

In 2009, she used her desktop publishing skills to lay out the stories and photos of our parents' anniversary book—another manifestation of her creative ability.

#

It's hard to imagine growing up as an only child, as my husband or a few of my friends have. While it's true that an only child does not have to share toys or clothes, they miss the companionship that I had, and also some of the chaos. We share memories, if not always the same opinions, but that's what made our home so interesting, and at times challenging. We wore hand-me-down clothing, and not necessarily in order of age. We played music and listened to Bill Cosby's hilarious stories on a certain record.

We laugh over some of those antics now, the eggs in the

haymow, looking for hidden away kittens. We share stories, from reminiscences of pets, through chasing after runaway cows while the school bus drives down the road, and our efforts to be paid for picking mustard in the grain field, to the remembrance of trips to Ipperwash each year. And we're there for each other, to offer consolation and support, in times of trouble.

Oh Brother!

When my youngest sister was eight and I was just past 21, my parents saw a picture of two little boys in the adoption column in the newspaper. They read the column as they had done on other occasions but this time with renewed interest. After much consideration, Mom and Dad decided that they had enough love and means to support another child, or in this case, two boys, aged 6 and 8.

By the time my parents applied to the agency and the paper work was begun, those two boys had a home. Mom still remembers their names. The social worker said there were more children needing a home; they would find a little boy for my parents.

A social worker came to our home to do a case study. She inspected our home, and asked many questions, including why my parents wanted to adopt. Within three months, the woman had found a little boy she thought was a good match. He had blonde hair, like several of us, and he had blue eyes to fit in with a blue-eyed family. His name was Wayne.

Mom and Dad had several visits with the social worker and this little boy. One of them was at a children's amusement park. Just before Wayne's first encounter with my parents, the worker had told him he would meet people interested in adopting him. When they met, Mom said that Wayne took Dad's hand, looked at him and said, "You're going to be my new Dad."

Wayne came to our home with his social worker for visits, and when he felt more comfortable, he stayed overnight, and later for a weekend. Early in the summer of his sixth year, Wayne came to live with us. This little blonde-haired dynamo quivered with energy and nervousness.

Mom put a lot of other commitments on hold that year—including her volunteer work for the Agricultural Society—so that she could devote the time and energy that Wayne needed to settle in and adjust to his new life with our family.

Just after Labour Day every year, my parents headed to the fairgrounds early on the Friday morning and spent the day setting up the displays in the arena, and in Dad's case, setting up bleachers and rings for the horse show.

This particular morning, Dad drove out the lane in the car, while Wayne rode on the tractor with Mom. Wayne saw him leave.

"He won't come back." He trembled and tears gathered in his eyes. In his young life, people had already left him behind.

"You'll see, he'll be back," Mom reassured him.

It must have been a long day for Wayne, but he learned it was true. His new father did come back. That wasn't the end of his anxieties and troubles, however. Still, he declared on his sixth birthday, at the lawyer's office, that he wanted to stay with his new family.

Since I was away teaching at the time, I have to rely on stories that my parents or siblings share. Mom told me that one day, during a long dry spell in summer, she had sent Wayne out give the garden plants a good long drink of water. The hose was connected to an outdoor tap, and with the extensions, it was quite long. It snaked diagonally across the lawn and lay across our country lane, so that the far end of the hose was out in the garden.

The pastor drove in, car windows down, and Wayne, in his glee, turned the hose on him. Wayne says that he sprayed the pastor for running over the hose.

Somewhat damp, the pastor headed for the kitchen where Mom was cooking lunch and told her what Wayne had done. He said, "I'd like to see him when he's a teenager." And the pastor, father of four sons of his own, laughed, as Mom does when she retells the story.

Mom, who'd never been called by the school about the misbehaviour of her five daughters, got to know the principal really well, through numerous phone calls and trips to the school. Sitting at a desk for minutes, if not hours, proved to be very difficult for Wayne. He loved to talk and here was an audience who listened—even when he got in trouble for it. It was an issue he faced all through his school life.

A small boy and the church choir

Wayne was quite young when Mom and Dad started taking him to church. My parents had always sat in the balcony when we were small, and they continued to do so, while Wayne sat downstairs with the Sunday school children and their teachers, until it was time for them to go to their classes.

One Sunday, everything was going as usual with the service, and the choir was singing the anthem in the loft at the back of the church. Mom and Dad sensed people looking at them. Parishioners looked from them to downstairs, and then back up at them.

Suspecting it had something to do with Wayne, they peered over the railing to see what he was up to. To their horror, he was standing on the seat, facing backwards towards the choir, and moving his arms as if he were directing them!

Very funny if it's not your child! Mom and Dad stopped going to church on a weekly basis as they couldn't face the embarrassment and Wayne's unpredictable shenanigans. Joan says that after that Sunday, Mom and Dad would take turns, with one of them staying home with Wayne, and the other taking her and Kim to church and Sunday school. It's a story they can laugh about now.

Coming home to visit

My brother lives across country now and only comes home once a year or so, but we keep in touch. These days, he's six-foot something and calls me his little sister, while he laughs and uses me for a leaning post. He calls Mom and Dad on their birthdays, their wedding anniversary, and Christmas, and he still calls for advice.

We picked him up at our nearby airport on one such visit and brought him to our place for an overnight stay before our family gathering the next day. We exchanged hugs, and he shook hands with my husband. Wayne was glad to be off the confining space in the airplane and through the waiting times such journeys impose on passengers. He also desperately needed a cigarette.

He talked all the way to our house, including a cell phone call back to Alberta, reminding someone to take care of his cat while he was gone.

"Could we stop at Tim's? I'm ready for a cup of coffee."

I assured Wayne that Len was good at making coffee and that dinner was waiting. Perhaps we could go to Tim Hortons before he returned home.

Wayne wolfed down the roast beef dinner, as if he hadn't eaten in days.

"I prefer it to my own cooking," he quipped. He told us that he cooked over a hot plate since his oven wasn't working, and that our beef dinner was very good. He was into seconds before I finished my first, and he enjoyed the chocolate cheesecake too.

"I can't take credit for the dessert," I said. "Say thanks to Zehrs for that."

He remembered Mom's birthday and worried aloud that he had missed her eightieth celebration. "Could we go to Zehrs?" he asked. "How long would it take to decorate a cake? I want to take one along tomorrow."

"Mom's eightieth is next year," I said.

"Are you sure?"

"Yes, it's still coming, but we can get a cake anyway."

And so he and my husband drove to the grocery store and got a cake. We'd deliver it the next day when we got together for our family Christmas.

Wayne slept soundly in our spare room that night, having taken care of something important.

Mom and Dad had arranged the visit, and my husband and I were the only other ones who knew he was coming. My sisters, brothers-in-law, nieces and nephews and our adult children were very surprised and happy to see him, and Wayne seemed glad to be home with us.

The next few days of Wayne's stay were full of visits, dinners, movie nights and sleepovers with various members of the family, until it was time to leave for the airport. Wayne took along some new sweaters, a gift card for Tim Hortons, and a cup of coffee to go.

Home is wherever one feels comfortable, I suppose. For Wayne, coming home may be as emotionally charged as when he first came, sometimes feeling like he belongs and sometimes not. He has a good job where he lives now, and he works hard.

Although we can never know how it feels to be in his shoes, we have learned something beyond our familiar life, and we can be more sympathetic to others who have known uncertainty in their young lives. There is no doubt that Wayne has also learned from us. Though there are times we want to say "Oh, brother!" we love him and care about him very much.

My Grandparents

Two sets of grandparents

I had two sets of grandparents. We called both grandmas Grandma and both grandpas Grandpa. My mother's youngest brother, Jackie, came along for visits with his parents for some time, and so we called them Grandma and Grandpa with Jackie. The other set were Grandma and Grandpa, because it was just the two of them. So readers will not be confused, I will refer to my paternal grandparents as Grandpa Ted and Grandma Flora, and my maternal grandparents as Grandpa Bill and Grandma Ardena.

Grandpa Ted and Grandma Flora

Grandpa Ted and Grandma Flora lived in Stratford, in a clean and tidy bungalow on East Gore Street. Sometimes we visited them after a Friday evening shopping trip in the city, a rare treat, or on a Sunday afternoon. Grandpa Ted was a serious man who never seemed to laugh much. He wore wire-rimmed spectacles that seemed to magnify his serious blue eyes, and he read a lot, especially the newspaper. Grandma Flora, on the other hand, smiled often, showing off the twinkle in her eyes that reminded me of Dad. She had a soft lap for cuddling and paid attention to youngsters who visited.

I remember one such visit on a summer evening. Mom and Dad had taken us shopping, then we stopped in at their house for a visit. Wearing a good school dress and a new fuzzy blue sweater, I kneeled on the rug next to their coffee table and looked at the photos and postcards in albums, our grandparents' souvenir of a trip out West. There were pictures of trains travelling along the tracks through white-capped mountains, with goats on the hills, lakes tucked between mountain peaks, and the most beautiful blue sky with hardly a cloud. Pictures of the inside of the train showed people sitting at tables, eating dinner, and all the time the train was hurrying through the mountains. I learned those were the Rocky Mountains, and I wanted to go on a train ride too.

When we knew my grandparents were coming to visit us, we watched for their silver gray Corvair coming down the road. Grandpa drove slowly so the tires wouldn't kick up the gravel and chip the paint of their new car, the car that one day would be mine.[7]

    Having lived and worked on the land that became our farm, Grandpa was always interested in seeing the crops and talking about farming, fertilizer, and prices of wheat or corn. He and Dad took slow walks across the yard and to the field. They'd talk, while Grandma chatted with our mother.

My grandparents went to Florida for several winters, so we didn't see them for at least three months at a time. Grandpa found the cold hard to bear, yet he missed his family, and Grandma went wherever he was comfortable, though she probably enjoyed the warm weather too. When they came back, they were tanned and

---

[7] - See "What a Car!" - *p. 137*

we were white-skinned, and they had two summers every year. Grandma Flora loved to sew and often brought back fabric for new dresses for my sisters and me.[8]

#

I remember coming home from school one day and seeing Grandma sitting at the quilting frame making tiny, even stitches. Other quilters had been there that day, but Grandma Flora had stayed longer and was still sewing. The quilt depicted rows of sailboats, and it was for the bed that Mary and I shared. When the quilt was done, I often traced those stitches and lines with my fingers and thought what a grand quilt it was.

I remember, too, a family New Year's gathering. There was a piano in the hall and Grandma asked me to play a song for her. I was shy and feeling quite nervous about making mistakes with so many people in that room. I didn't play, though I often wished I had, since I never got another chance.

#

I learned while working on this book that Grandma Flora had grown up on a farm only a country block from where I grew up, and that she had moved to the city with her family in her teen years and got a job working for Duggan's Department Store in the

---

[8] - See "Anticipated Visits" - *p. 148*

special order department. While she worked there, she became very skilled in sewing and hat-making.

Ted had grown up and gone to school in the city. After public school, he had started to work for the Canadian National Railroad (CNR), where his father worked. Ted had worked hard and had a responsible job in the CNR shop.

Ted and Flora and their families attended the same church and were active members there. Their family speculates that Flora and Ted met at church, possibly when they sang in the choir together.

Ted's grandfather, Samuel, born in Switzerland, came first to the United States and then to Canada. He bought a farm in South Easthope Township where he and his wife raised their family. When Samuel died, Ted's father, John, moved with his family to the city, thinking that he could support a family more easily there. He got a job working for the railway.

I find it interesting that Grandpa Ted, a city boy, eventually moved to a farm. Perhaps Ted's grandfather had more influence on his grandson than he thought.

#

Knowing that the gases produced in the CNR shop were a problem for Ted's breathing, he and Flora decided to buy a farm. When they moved to the country, Ted studied agricultural trends in farming magazines and newspapers and attended lectures at the Ontario Agricultural College, a division of the present University of Guelph. Ted practised crop rotation before it was general practice, adding mulch to the soil, and perceiving that fertilizer would bring better crop yields, he used it on his own crops, and promoted it among his neighbours.

My father says that Grandpa told him of concerns he had with the flooding each year, so that some areas could not be cultivated. Grandpa had done a lot of reading and listening and eventually determined that the land could be tiled. My father says, "When this was done, the land would be as good as or better than a lot of the higher land in the area."

More on Grandpa Ted

The spring after Grandma Flora died, Grandpa Ted moved into the new house they had built on the sideroad near our farm. He later remarried and enjoyed some companionship until his second wife, Jennie, was also diagnosed with cancer and died. After a year or so of living in the city again, he decided to move to Florida for good. I visited him there once with my friend Linda, before either of us was married.

I took pictures while we were there. Grandpa Ted in front of his home, tanned, slimmer than when we had last seen him, a little less hair on his head, and that same serious expression on his face. There were also pictures of the tourist spots we saw together.

"I didn't remember that your hair was red," he said one day.

"It isn't, usually," I answered. My sister, Mary, who was a hairdresser, had tinted it, and my natural red highlights made it look as red as a strawberry blonde.

A few years later, my husband and I travelled to the United

States for some months after our wedding. We spent time with Grandpa and went sightseeing together. It was hard to leave his home when we stopped in again after a side trip to Key West. I didn't know when we'd get back again.

December 8, 1975, is the date of the only letter I have from Grandpa Ted, from his home in Lakeland, Florida, responding to my Christmas card and letter. I had given him the news about our expected baby, due the coming spring.

He wrote, "I am happy for you both in the event you are looking forward to in April."

Having gone where the warm climate was more comfortable for his arthritis and his breathing, he missed us and welcomed visitors and letters from home and family. He often told us when we called at Christmas that we should come to see him again.

Every year, Grandpa sent his adult family members a gift subscription to *Reader's Digest*, a tangible gift for the whole family that lasted all year every year for as long as he lived away from us. He loved to read and obviously appreciated the magazine.

He continued on the one-page letter, saying that "Brian, George's boy," had driven down to Florida with a group of friends. Grandpa thought it was an Oldsmobile that Brian drove. My cousin, Brian, who would have been about 19 years old at the time, had grown quite a bit since Grandpa moved to Florida, for Grandpa Ted remarks "what a big boy he is now."

Ever a man of the land, knowing that the right amount of warmth and sufficient rainfall are important to good crops, Grandpa wrote that they'd had a little bit of "so-called winter" with temperatures of 50 degrees (F) at night and in the daytime "close to 75 to 80." He had only been there a few years, but he knew from reading the newspaper and talking with folks that they'd had a relatively dry five years.

One thought seems to flow into the next and Grandpa moves from the weather and looking forward to warmth, then he signs off, "So long" and "Love, Your Grandad," with his signature at the bottom, in remarkably steady handwriting for his 85 years.

We sent Grandpa Ted a birth announcement the next April when our daughter was born, and he generously sent a cheque that we might use for her, which we deposited into her first bank account.

A year later, and just over a month after our daughter's first birthday, we learned of my grandfather's sudden passing at his home in Lakeland. Arrangements were made to send his body home, and we gathered for our final goodbye on a warm day in early June.

And so we laid my Grandpa Ted to rest—a man whom I had come to know better as an adult and whom I would learn even more about while editing a family history project for my parents. Grandpa Ted was a man who thought carefully and studied things before getting into them. In that way, we are a lot alike. Grandpa Ted had an insatiable love for the land, as my father does, and a love of reading, a lifelong habit that kept him abreast of new developments long after he stopped farming. He was a man both in tune with the times and ahead of them too.

Grandpa Bill and Grandma Ardena

Grandpa Bill and Grandma Ardena lived on a farm near Shakespeare when I was growing up. We'd turn off the highway and drive up the gravelled lane, lined by several fir trees, and park around the back of their home, a hip-roofed structure, covered with green siding.[9] We always entered the house by the back door.

#

Sometimes, while Mom and Grandma visited, my sisters and I went to the workshop to see what Great Uncle Edward was doing. We were allowed to sit on a high stool and watch, as long as we promised not to touch anything. I loved the smell of wood shavings and I liked to watch him carve things out of a block of wood, but watching is harder than doing it ourselves, so we moved on to other fun after some minutes of watching and talking with him.[10]

If Grandpa was out in the barn when we visited, we went out to say hello, and to see the horses. Inside that black barn, Grandpa also kept cattle, pigs, and chickens. On the upper level, reached by a sloped bank, my grandfather stored the hay, straw and grain.

At the end of the barn was the small white-washed milk house where the milk was stored and the milking equipment was kept.

---

[9] - See "One Last Moonlight" - *p. 170*

[10] - See "His Own Way" - *p. 161*

In spring and summer, the animals spent most of their days in the fields. I remember Grandpa walking out to the field, cap pulled low over his head, to bring the cows in for milking.

The CN railway tracks crossed the back of my grandparents' property. Mom said that one time when the Queen came to Canada to visit, they went out to the field to watch for her. As the train passed, they waved, and—so the story goes—the Queen actually waved back.

#

Grandma Ardena was just over five feet tall, her face quite round. Her wavy blue-tinted white hair was always neat. No one fooled with Grandma when she meant business, but she had a good sense of humour too that I later learned to appreciate. Mom said that her mother sewed clothes for her children, and when someone outgrew their clothing, she remade them to fit the younger children.

In my time with Grandma Ardena, I watched her sew both patchwork and crazy quilts as well as tied comforters. She tatted edges for pillowslips and crocheted the most intricate doilies. She once tried to teach me to crochet as well.[11]

#

---

[11] - See "Crochet Lessons" - *p. 153*

Grandpa Bill's walk slowed as his limp became more pronounced, an effect of the polio that he contracted as a young man. Never a man given to excess talk, he nevertheless enjoyed life. He took time to rest, often napping after lunch with a newspaper over his face so that any flies that got into the house wouldn't disturb him.

Later, when they retired from farming, we visited their home in town. Grandpa Bill had a habit of tickling us until we were giddy with laughter just before it was time for us to go home to bed. I remember him, too, relaxing in his easy chair, reading the paper, with smoke circling off his pipe and up to the ceiling. When there was a roomful of people visiting, Grandpa often shut off his hearing aid because it amplified all the noise. A big family meant lots of people coming and going.

#

When I worked in the nursing home in town one summer, I lived with Grandma Ardena and Grandpa Bill, and I got to know them much better. On evenings that I wasn't working, Grandma and I sat in the dining room, where the light was good. She crocheted or tatted while I worked on my hand-hooked rug, and we talked or just enjoyed being together. Sometimes I stayed with Grandpa while Grandma walked uptown to get a few groceries or went to have coffee with a friend. After working hard for so many years, and being somewhat older than my Grandmother, it seemed that Grandpa just wanted to relax at home.

When Grandma and I cooked together, she often made pancakes, which she pronounced "panacakes." She loved Limburger cheese and tried to get me to taste it, but I couldn't get past the smell. Though she was of English background, she had worked out at other homes as a young girl out of school and that was probably where she learned to make the German dishes that Grandpa loved. I remember that she was an excellent cook and baker. She could put on a great meal for themselves or for guests, which they entertained by the tableful.

The kitchen in town was a little smaller than the one on the farm, but the window ledges in that bright room were full of flowers, especially in the summer. I remember a sign that hung in her kitchen: "No matter where I serve my guests, it seems they like my kitchen best." It was true, since we often talked in the kitchen while we cooked or cleaned up dishes, and even afterwards when we could be sitting in the living room.

#

I was so lucky to have known both sets of grandparents—to know their love and to spend time with them. From them, I learned patience, persistence, duty, love and faith. Lessons they lived every day of their lives, that they passed on to their children, and that I have tried to incorporate into my own life.

Part II
Farm Life

Risks of Farming

Mom and Dad planted their crops in hopes that the corn and grain would grow and yield, that there would be food for the animals housed there, that stock would bring in a good price, and that the garden, carefully planted and tended, would feed hungry mouths in the family, the community, and beyond.

Farm life is for those willing to work hard, and for those who love the land. The only commute to work involves driving the tractor to the field to plant or harvest, and taking stock or crops to market.

Our farm neighbours are also part of the package; neighbours whose turnip crops we hoed or whose raspberries we picked when they needed help; neighbours who were involved in agricultural pursuits, selling fertilizer or seed corn; the Amish families, with their horses and buggies, who lived among us for a time, and people we still see, but only at the agricultural fair, who are a part of the wider community.

My parents have volunteered in the community and the church, demonstrated the value of working together, shared with the less fortunate, and invited neighbours to pick produce from the abundance of our garden.

Though not without its challenges, it has been a good life, and my childhood on the farm was overall a happy one—a way of life that taught me the value of spending wisely and being thrifty, the certainty of the seasonal cycles of planting and tending crops, and the pleasure of savouring the fruits of the earth, the results of hard work. These were all life lessons that years later, in our home in the city, I sought to pass down to my own children.

Dare to Ride

My sisters and I begged for a horse. We had cows, pigs, chickens, and cats on our farm, and a dog that followed us everywhere, so in our eyes, having a horse would make the farm complete. After a good deal of pleading, we got a pony instead. Dad agreed to board this pony with the permission of the owner, that we might ride it sometimes. Dad had grown up on the farm having work horses, so he knew how to handle them. The owner agreed, but he warned us that Ginger had quite a temper.

Dad said we had to let the pony settle in first, but on the day we were to finally ride her, Mary volunteered to go first. Dad supervised the getting on, and he adjusted the saddle and stirrup. Mary rode Ginger in a circle around the gravelled barnyard, with Dad close by.

The pony had not bucked like the rodeo horses I saw on television, nor had she refused the rider a short jaunt across the barnyard. My sister beamed as she dismounted.

Bonnie was next. Dad helped her up and she settled in the saddle, with her feet in the stirrups. She sat up tall, ready for her ride. With Dad guiding, the pony moved forward, crossed the yard, and back to where Mary and I stood.

I convinced myself that Ginger was a safe bet. No more dangerous than riding my bicycle.

Dad helped me up, as he had done for my sisters. I sat in the saddle and planted my feet in the stirrups, which he adjusted once again. With my one hand holding the rein and the other gripping the saddle horn, Ginger and I started out. She plodded a short distance then headed for the barn door. Just outside the stable, Ginger dipped her head low and kicked up her hind feet.

I hung on tight, but I was not nearly as brave as those rodeo riders. Ginger kicked again and lowered her head, and I was on my way to the ground, flying clear over her head. It happened so fast that I barely recall the landing, only that I hurt.

Shaking from the fall, I got up from the ground. My hands, arms, knees, and shins were scraped and bleeding. I decided that the horses and ponies on a merry-go-round were far safer, even as Ginger refused another rider that day. She may have given rides at other times, but I never tried to ride her again.

#

When I was in college, I stayed overnight with a classmate at her home in the city. Carol is an avid rider, and she asked if I'd like to go riding with her. No braver than when the pony threw me, and thinking that horses are bigger and therefore more dangerous, I resisted. I told her of my experience, and she insisted that the horse was well-behaved.

I couldn't do it; I didn't want to be dumped again, from higher up this time. I also had more to lose, like days off work if I broke any bones. Fortunately, she accepted my feelings and pressed no further.

I have since learned that ponies are far more temperamental than horses. Carol may have been right after all, that the horses at the stable were quite gentle.

If a friend ever asks me to go horseback riding again, I might have to reconsider.

Farm Pets

Because we lived in the country, we always had a dog and at least a family of cats. No animals were allowed in the house; they had to stay in the barn or the garage, except for the one time when Bonnie insisted that her Persian cat needed to be in the house. Bonnie, the sometime veterinarian, must have caught Mom at a weak moment.

The vacuum cleaner never got a holiday, nor did the person operating it. The hair problem got worse when the cat developed hairballs. The cat would sit there and choke and cough. We thought she was dying, but she'd sputter out a wad of hair and go on with her grooming. In spite of medicine from the vet, the cat died. Ever after, all four-legged pets were banished to the barn, or the garage, but Bonnie never gave up on her mission to doctor pets back to health.

Tippy, a little white dog with rust-colored spots, and one of a number of dogs we had over the years, slept on an old coat on the cement landing in the garage. He followed us everywhere: out the lane to get the mail, to the barn when we did chores, and to the field when we brought the cows in for milking. He followed us across the road to 'the fifty'—the title we gave the 50 acres across the road—when Mom sent us out to call Dad for dinner.

Tippy could have slept in the barn near the other animals, but he preferred the garage. He cut his teeth on boots or shoes that were left behind, and he'd follow, tail wagging, to the backyard when someone emerged with a dish of leftovers. He knew where his next meal came from.

It was Kim who named the animals, even the chickens. "I don't think anyone else in our family was as concerned as I was that the chickens in the barn did not have names," she said. "How was one to tell which was which?"

There was a far bigger challenge waiting in the barn—naming successive litters of kittens hidden in the haymow. Once found, the mother hid them in a new place, and the hunt was on to find them again. The kittens were too cute and cuddly to leave alone. We tamed them eventually and brought them to the house to show our mother how cute they were—a temptation long before Kim was born.

Kim says, "These cats, once tamed, much to Mom's chagrin, would meow loudly and incessantly at the kitchen door for food or attention." Quite often, one would dash through our legs and run into the house, and we'd have to play a game of catch the kitten.

#

I lost track of the cats when I went away to college, but Kim updated me on their comings and goings. There was John, who used unsuspecting people's laps for his outhouse; Radsy, the wanderer, "who had more titles than the Queen of England and all of her ancestors put together"; and Fleabags, who "had about a hundred litters at Aunt Doris and Uncle Ed's farm" and more after she came to live with us.

Fleabags may have been a wanderer, but she had more roles to fill. We watched with amazement one day as Fleabags put up with Kim dressing her in doll clothes and putting her in the baby carriage. The cat would "valiantly crawl out of the carriage only to be scooped up and put back in again."

Our pets added to the fun with their quirks and antics, crawling in and out of our makeshift tents on the lawn in the middle of the night, or following us when we had a dish of food. Though our pets are long gone, and Kim has new ones at her home in town, it's still amusing to hear her talk about her experiences with them.

Entertainment

When I was growing up, the entertainment we enjoyed was usually of the inexpensive variety and close to home. With animals to feed, eggs to gather, and cows to milk morning and night, social activities took place between those hours of early morning and evening chores, or after evening chores, and since most other residents of our neighbourhood also lived on farms, entertaining guests or going out on Sunday afternoons worked out well for almost everyone. Evening activities like dances, community gatherings, roller skating at the arena, or trick or treating on Hallowe'en started after 7:30 or 8 pm, so that people living on farms could get their chores done.

Sunday, a Day of Rest

On Sundays, we took a day of rest from work in the fields and the garden, though farm animals still required care and food, eggs still had to be gathered and cows brought in for milking. We attended church and Sunday school regularly, being active members of our congregation.

On Sunday afternoons, we often visited with friends, neighbours or family, grandparents, aunts, uncles and cousins, or we invited others over for Sunday dinner or an afternoon visit. Still there were plenty of Sundays that we spent at home with our own family.

In summer, our trip to Ipperwash was a special event we looked forward to all year; it always occurred on a Sunday.

Summer Vacations

Since summer is the time of harvest, few farm owners take vacations at that time of year. In fact, the real reason for children having summers off in rural Canada was so that they could help their parents with harvest. July and August are the busiest months for farm families, though some crops like strawberries ripen in June, and field corn ripens as late as October.

Farm families rely on the harvest for food in winter: hay and grain crops for cattle, pigs and chickens. For we of the human race, garden produce such as peas, potatoes, onions and carrots, as well as apples, pears and cherries from the orchard, all reach their peak between July and August. Crops must be harvested when the commodities are at their peak of ripeness and must be handled and stored carefully for best quality.

The adage "All work and no play make Jack a dull boy" is reasonable. Just as a doctor and pastor put their social life on hold when there is an urgent need for their services, my parents took time for relaxation and a social life and allowed us the same, just not at the expense of getting the essential tasks done. There was always work that could be done, but the human body needs a rest. My parents recognized that and welcomed the break too.

We went for Sunday drives in summer, hiked in the closest national park a few hours' drive from home, went to a zoo, had picnic lunches at roadside parks, went to the beach, and attended family reunions, where we played baseball with our extended family.

Winter

In winters, before the front fields were retiled, we often skated on surfaces where water collected after fall rains and then froze. We also skated in our local arena on a Sunday afternoon, between hockey practices and league games. A special memory, however, is of skating and sliding on our rink at home, which we did for several years.

We tramped down the snow in an area Dad marked off by boards, and then we helped Dad flood the space with water each night until the ice layer was sufficiently thick and hard to endure skating. It could take a good week or more to get it ready, depending upon the weather and temperature.

As a finishing touch, Dad set up lights on poles around the rink so we could skate in the evening, and he set out straw bales alongside the rink so we had a place to sit whenever we needed a break or to put on or take off our skates. We shot cast-off pucks in our own game of hockey or just skated around the rink when friends came over to visit. Mom rarely came out to skate with us and preferred to treat us to hot chocolate and cookies afterwards.

Indoor fun

I trace my love of doing jigsaw puzzles back to assembling puzzles around the kitchen table. I remember a certain 1,000-piece puzzle—a picture of a Chinese pagoda—that took some time to assemble. Working on puzzles was a great way to pass a rainy or snowy afternoon. It could also be a test of patience at times when many pieces looked so similar, but it was pleasing when we finally put in the last piece.

Mom and Dad still do puzzles every winter and when we visit, I cannot resist the urge to add pieces to what is already completed.

Games

We played board games too: Crokinole, checkers, Chinese Checkers, Parcheesi (a steeplechase game), and Snakes and Ladders. Of these, I liked Crokinole the best and now have a board and playing pieces of my own.

The challenge is to flick a wooden playing piece, or disc, across the board and past small posts to land in the centre "20" hole, but we also must try to knock opponent's pieces off the board. The player or team with the highest score wins the game.

Crokinole originated in our local community, with the earliest known wooden board made in Perth County in 1876. There are two boards named after Tavistock, Ontario, as well.

We also had a hockey game, made out of a light metal that looked like an ice rink with hockey players on it. We dropped the puck into the centre ice and then maneuvered players by pushing and pulling levers at each end. It was a lot of fun but hard work too. If we were well coordinated and could make our men work, we might score a goal in the other person's net.

Our parents taught us card games too; we played as a family and with our friends. We learned the rules of rummy, snap, war, and eventually euchre, a family favourite, though I prefer Black Queens in cards, and Scrabble, a later addition to our game collection.

A Piano

Mom and Dad invested in a piano so that we girls could take music lessons. I think our first one was a Heintzman. It was a full-sized piano made from dark brown burnished wood, with matching stool. I started taking lessons when I was seven years old, at which time my feet could not yet reach the pedals, nor could my fingers stretch enough to play an octave, but I wanted to learn.

Mom, remembering her short time of lessons as a young girl, wanted to give us the opportunity to learn so we could play just for enjoyment. We were never asked to take exams, only to practise faithfully each week between lessons. Piano recitals were not common at the time in our community, but we played our pieces for our family and visitors and other times or places when we were asked.

I enjoyed my lessons and had certain favourite songs that I played long after I learned them, and that I played so many times that my family probably got tired of hearing them. God Save the Queen, our national anthem, was one of those early much practised pieces, but I had favourite hymns too.

Practising was not a chore for me, but was time to myself with the piano. My sisters were not allowed to come and play at the end of the keyboard during my practice time and each of us respected that rule.

When we had company, our parents asked us to play our pieces, and we also played for the occasional Women's Institute meetings while Mom was a member, as well as at school talent nights. Sometimes Mary and I played duets that we worked on in our lessons with our teacher; it was a challenge, but an enjoyable one.

About once a year, the piano needed tuning. Our piano tuner was a man who lived in Stratford. He had little or no vision but knew how to tune and play a piano. Dad would pick him up in the morning and bring him to our home for a good part of the day. The man would tune the piano, then play it while we listened eagerly, and he'd have supper with us before Dad took him home.

Television

Our home entertainment choices changed the day my parents brought home our first television set. I was about eight years old at the time. We could get only a few channels and needed an antenna on the house roof to bring in even those few stations.

I remember Mary and I coming home from school to see the end of Howdy Doody, a children's show with puppets that Bonnie was watching intently. The Friendly Giant began the same year and continued until the 80s, but we could only watch that on holidays. Still it was one of my favourite shows, even when I grew past other children's television programs.

Mary and I would get home just in time to watch Lassie, a weekly show about a boy and his dog and their adventures. After the show was over, Mom turned off the set and either sent us outdoors to play or gave us tasks in the kitchen, like setting the table for dinner.

Popular television shows

Weekends were the best time for television. We enjoyed Ponderosa, a weekly saga of a ranching family, starring Lorne Greene as a single father raising his sons; and Roy Rogers and Dale Evans who, no matter what drama played out on their show, always rode off into the sunset on their horses, singing "Happy trails... ," which I sang along with them as the credits rolled on the screen.

On Wednesday evenings in the fall and winter, we girls sat around the kitchen table doing our homework until Hockey Night in Canada began. Dad, being an avid hockey player and sports fan, usually just finished his chores in time to clean up and relax in his favourite chair when the program started at 8 pm. Still sitting around the kitchen table, we watched the television that sat on a shelf in the corner of the kitchen. We cheered our favourite players on when they made a goal in the opposing team's net. Although Dad appreciated quite a number of players, his smile grew wider whenever Gordie Howe scored a goal.

Mom and Dad eventually moved the television to the living room, where we'd gather on the sofa or sit on the rug to watch, and while television never ruled our activities, we did have our favourite shows.

On the Sunday evenings that we were at home, after supper dishes and chores were done, we watched The Ed Sullivan Show, a weekly entertainment program for families that started before we had television and ran for nearly two decades. The show was hosted by Ed Sullivan, an entertainment columnist with a great flair for dramatic introductions. In fact, he was called a Toastmaster. The show featured dance and magic acts, acrobatics, and circus clips. Comedy acts, a consistent feature of the program, included Red Skelton, a hobo clown; Milton Berle; and Jack Benny with the violin he couldn't play. Popular singers included Elvis Presley, an early appearance by the Beatles, as well as other pop groups and soloists.

Front Page Challenge, with host Fred Davis and regular panelists Gordon Sinclair, Pierre Berton and Betty Kennedy, started as a summer quiz show—to identify a major newsmaker, the weekly mystery guest. The show was so popular that it continued until 1995. We may not have always guessed the mystery guest correctly, but we learned about world culture and politics by watching the show.

#

While we had much to do around the farm, in addition to our school activities and homework, and Mom and Dad had their weekly and seasonal work, and responsibilities as parents, farm owners and community volunteers, we all looked forward to those favourite activities, whether they were assembling jigsaw puzzles, watching television, skating, playing baseball with friends, or visiting with others. We enjoyed the time away from work, relaxed and rejuvenated for the day or week ahead.

Errands with Dad

Kim accompanied Dad on important farm errands, one of which was going to the stockyards. Sometimes they'd buy fruit and vegetables from market vendors, and other times they took a hog to market. If Kim tagged along when animals went to market, she'd probably say goodbye to them by name. Aside from the stock and produce, she remembers the tasty home-made cream puffs they bought.

Being in the farming business, there was another important place to go, especially with old equipment that continually broke down. Dad was handy and could make a lot of things work, but sooner or later, he had to take a jaunt to Harley's to pick up a new part for the combine or the seeder, but mostly the combine, as I remember. The trips were not limited to just picking up parts. They provided an opportunity to socialize and talk shop.

Kim accompanied Dad on quite a few trips to the implement dealers. She said, "I would have enjoyed it much more if the visits had been short and sweet, but once Dad started talking parts, gears and motors, it would take forever to get out of there."

One day she volunteered to stay in the truck and wait for Dad there. She figured if Dad knew she was sitting out in the truck, he would be really quick to finish his business. But it didn't work out the way she hoped, and it was a long, long wait. After that, she just went with him and resigned herself to waiting around while he chatted.

Kim remembers the toy model of an International dump truck that Dad purchased on one of these trips and says that after all these years, her favourite colour is still red—International Red.

Pump Stories

Outside the kitchen window
two boys with as much energy to burn
as stories to tell
one pulls the pump handle
the other holds the pail
up and down   up and down
water splashes into the bucket
sprays summer-tanned bare legs
with wash water for the kitchen floor

Off to the pasture
where cows and horses await a drink
the stories match our steps
tall tales too farfetched to believe
but still I listened

"Bet'cha can't pump" they say

I wrestle with the handle
up and down   up and down
muscles burn with the effort
but there's no giving up

We fill the trough, one pail after another
then dally on our return
more stories for our steps
hoping the floor will be dry

Whitewashing the Barn

Mom and Dad filled our summers with jobs, to keep us busy and out of trouble. The summer I was 14, the barn on our farm needed some attention. The boards had turned a dull weathered gray, bearing little resemblance to the bright red it had been years before. My parents decided they couldn't afford to hire a painter that year. Instead, they delegated my sister Mary and me to help with the job.

Our paint consisted of a mixture of lime and water; we'd whitewash the barn instead.

I do not like heights. I wouldn't climb an eight-foot ladder or get in a bucket loader to pick apples, yet saying no to whitewashing the barn wasn't a choice; I had to help. Mary, on the other hand, seemed to look forward to getting up there and doing it.

We wouldn't be climbing ladders. For that I was glad, because the barn was huge—a two-storey monstrosity. Instead, Dad built a wooden platform with rails around it. He secured the platform to the loader on his biggest tractor. I cringed as I watched him load it.

"It's safe," Dad assured me, but I doubted it.

The whitewash mix was ready too, and Dad's jeans and shirt already bore some specks of the lime. His cap and his dark hair showed signs of it too.

Mary and I were 'on duty,' as Mom would say, to paint the barn. With the loader on the ground, we climbed into the stage, a bucket of whitewash and brushes between us. Dad climbed on the tractor and started the action. Up, up, we went. My knuckles turned white from hanging on so tight, as Dad lifted the loader with a tilting action, up, up and back, up and back.

Dad lifted the stage as high as it would go and locked the loader in place, then he drove as close to the side of the barn as he dared, which was never close enough for my liking. Mary didn't seem to mind the height, but I stood with knees that felt like jelly, picked up the second brush, and dipped it into the pail of whitewash. EEu! The lime burned inside my nose, it was so strong, but Mary got right to the painting as if it didn't bother her.

We painted as far as we could reach, and that dry wood just sucked up the liquid like it hadn't had a drink in ages. What was whitewash going to do for those dry old boards anyway?

As I stood up there on that platform painting, I thought about Mark Twain's book *Tom Sawyer*, which our teacher had read to us that year. I remembered how Tom had to whitewash the fence and I felt some kinship with him. *At least he got to stand on the ground.*

With a gap between us and the barn boards, and my arms being shorter than my sister's, the distance I could cover was smaller. When I stopped thinking about Tom painting the fence, I worried about something letting go, and us falling suddenly onto the gravel below, never more to whitewash the barn, but it didn't happen. Dad's word was good, as usual. And there was no calling for artistry up there either, just a matter of covering those hungry old boards with this smelly stuff.

When we had painted all we could reach, we'd call Dad, who had to climb down the ladder from where he was painting, and move the tractor, the two of us hanging on. The process happened over and over and my father got lots of exercise going up and down the ladder. Between some of these moves, Mom brought us a cold drink, since we were soon as thirsty as those old boards, from working in the sun.

Finally, the job was done. We stood on the ground looking at this great white structure, still an old barn, but looking somewhat better. I had done it, in spite of my fear of heights, and the loader hadn't gone crashing to the ground. It would be a while before the job had to be done again, and with any luck, a younger sibling would get to do it the next time. It often seemed that whenever one task was completed, another one waited. That's the way it is on a farm; my parents must have felt that way too. Still, whitewashing the barn was a huge undertaking and Dad was pleased that it was well done.

Dad's Hired Hand

Before we older girls were mature enough to do chores in the house and barn unsupervised and when the youngest siblings were babies, Mom's duties in summer consisted mainly of looking after children, housework, picking vegetables from the garden, canning, and helping with a few of the barn chores. It was during this time that Mom and Dad had a hired man to work for them.

I remember Cecil, a tall thin man in his 50s, wearing overalls and a straw hat. He was friendly in a reserved sort of way, yet not overly talkative. He arrived early for morning chores, ate meals with us, and drove the tractor for scuffling, harrowing, seeding and harvest. About supper time, he'd drive out the lane with his old truck and head for home. Dad could handle evening chores, but not all the other work, by himself.

#

Later, as we were able, we girls took on more chores and could be trusted to do them or babysit the younger ones, so that Mom was freed up to take on a new role—driving the tractor in the field, either pulling the combine for grain harvesting or pulling the baler and wagon for bringing in the hay or straw from the field. She called herself Dad's hired hand.

#

Her skin got very tanned working out on the tractor like that. People would say she was as brown as a berry. I didn't know about brown berries. The berries we picked at home were either red or purple, except for the green gooseberries. Anyway, she was tanned while I burned.

There was a puzzle I had to work out, though. My mother and her sisters had some unusual nicknames, and it was a long time before I sorted out who belonged to which name. I could never figure out why my mother was called Aunty Chocolate by the nieces and nephews, even by her brothers.

Eventually, I asked and got a straight answer, along with a

laugh. It was Uncle Stuart, Mom's oldest brother, who had given her the name, and it was because her skin got so brown in the summer. She would have helped with outdoor work at home, especially in the garden, so he'd see how tanned she got every summer while his red hair got redder and his fair, freckled skin got more freckles and burned in the sun. He must have envied her ability to tan, but it was more likely his silly sense of humour that was responsible for the nickname.

As Mom gardened and drove tractor in summer, she tanned long before we hit the beach on our yearly trip to Ipperwash each August first weekend. There was no lying around in the sun on a farm.

The sun's rays were strong then too. When Mom worked in the field or the garden, she wore a babushka—a scarf tied around her head and tied in a knot at the top—like Aunt Jemima on the pancake mix packages. The babushka didn't protect her face and neck from the sun, but it covered her hair and scalp. Her tan looked good, but we didn't know what we know now about sunburn, though we were aware of the effects of heat and sunstroke.

One year, when Mary and I went to the Toronto Exhibition with my aunt and uncle, we each came home with a large sombrero with a high grooved top, and with our names embroidered on the crown. Around the wide brim was a row of turquoise pompoms that swayed as we walked; I thought they were really neat, for a time anyways. I seem to remember my hat lasting longer, but I don't remember why that was. Maybe the dog got hold of Mary's hat and chewed holes in it.

When the novelty wore off, I didn't wear the hat very much. It needed a string to keep the hat on my head. When working in the garden, the wide brim kept the sun off my face and the back of my neck, but it sometimes got in the way, and I didn't especially like the string under my chin. My hat was retired to the top of a closet for awhile.

Mom, becoming more conscious about the sun exposure on her face and neck, and perhaps after suffering a few uncomfortable burns, considered the sombrero. She asked one day if she might wear my hat to drive tractor for harvest. I knew how hot the sun beat down from helping with the haying; it was too big to wear for baling and would get in the way, but for sitting on a tractor for hours, the hat would provide some shade. I said sure, she may as well use it, and it became her hat.

I remember taking lunches and drinks out to the field and seeing Mom from far off wearing that wide-brimmed sombrero and thinking what a good thing it was for her. As long as the strings around her neck held, and the wind wasn't strong, she would be protected from the sun on those hot summer days.

The hat is long gone, as are the days when Mom drove the tractor for harvest. There's no photo of her wearing it either, for at the end of the day she would have been tired and dusty, and we would have been busy doing our chores. Even when she was done driving tractor for the day and cleaned up, there was still garden produce to can or freeze and there were children to send to bed. And the next day the process started all over again until it either rained, the combine broke down, or the harvest was done. Such were the busy days of harvest as Dad's "hired hand," and it seemed Mom was always up for the challenge.

From the Tractor Seat

An April wind dries the land
splashing my sun-starved face with coolness

ridged tires   as tall as me
scatter clods of earth
headland to headland
row after row
        two dozen silver spades
        slice grass-covered earth
        into wavy ribbon rows
exposing wriggling life
   to ragged screeching crows

Grain Harvest

The old combine eats its way
up and down crop rows
a hungry beast
with its mouth to the ground
severing stalk from root
combing seed from stem
with its scissor teeth
its belly filling with golden grain
tumbling chaff and straw
spitting out stems
for the baler to bind up
in a field of stubble

Frozen Weeds Were Goalposts

where corn grew tall   two seasons before
our open air arena   rippled and bumpy

we shot castoff pucks
past frosted clumps of earth
                          and shorn stalks
wobbly ankles on sharpened blade
laughing   cheering
'til jack frost bit
                our fingers and our noses

we skidded to our hay bale bench
shoved tingling toes into waiting boots
                      and hurried to a warm kitchen

C. R. Wilker

The Tavistock Agricultural Society and the Fall Fair

My earliest memory of the Fall Fair is marching in the parade with my school classmates and teacher, with two students holding our school banner for all to see. For many years, the parade ended on the fairgrounds, with people sitting in the bleachers, watching and cheering. The fair could not happen without community involvement and the dedication of members and organizers of the agricultural society.

The Tavistock Agricultural Society was formed on January 9, 1907, on the amalgamation of the East Zorra and South Easthope Agricultural Societies. The motto of the Tavistock Society is "Show what you grow … share what you know!"

My parents have both served on the Agricultural Society board and committees for many years, in the set up, organizing, and judging of events. Mom worked in Homecrafts, and Dad, with heavy and light horses.

Leadership

The society's leadership began with the men, but eventually the women saw a need to host their own division. My mother was the 1968–69 President of the Homecraft Division, the first year that the women had a section of their own. Encouraged by Eleanor Mosher, who assumed the Secretary role, they had to do some convincing, but they managed to bring it about. Every year since, there has been a new President of the society, a woman for the Homecraft Division and either a man or woman for the society at large.

Exhibits and prizes

The fair board, local business owners, organizations and the Women's Institutes of the area sponsor categories in home crafts, fresh and canned fruits and vegetables, arts, flowers, and children's school projects. There are also home-baked pies, cookies and cakes in glass display cases that judges must have enjoyed tasting.

Our 4-H Homemaking Club always set up a display each year, showing what we had learned, and we entered our sewing projects for judging in the Junior division.

Other 4-H clubs and adult members of the community met that day to show their calves, pigs or sheep and to be judged on their showmanship and the health of their animals. Crops such as corn, grains and hay have been judged, both the ones brought as exhibits, and also the standing crops, making it truly an agricultural fair.

#

The fair could be a noisy place, with cattle bawling, hawkers calling, midway music playing, loud speakers announcing the hunter and jumper shows, and people talking.

Later in the day was the tug-of-war competition. At one time, local baseball teams played under the lights when the horse show was over, and after the field was cleaned up, but for some years now, the popular entertainment on Saturday night has been the air band competition, which both young and old enjoy.

Fun at the Fair

The weekend of the Fall Fair arrives with the beginning of cooler weather and leaves changing colours. School begins that same week, doubling the excitement. The fair starts with a dance on Friday night—an event meant for teens and adults, and the same event at which my parents met just over 60 years ago.

On Saturday, we drive into town and park, before the police close the road to further traffic. We line up by the curb and wait for the parade to start. The fire trucks pass us first, blaring and tooting their horns. Following the fire trucks is the procession of local people driving tractors, some of the vehicles being of an impressive vintage. Horseback riders, wearing plaid shirts and jeans and cowboy hats or riding gear, wave to us from their trotting mounts.

We see costumed bicyclists, walkers and clowns, some carrying baskets of candies that they throw out to spectators at the roadside, or people pulling wagons with small children riding. The co-owner of Les and Hap's, our favourite ice cream place, rides down the centre line, wearing a top hat and tuxedo, on his high-wheeled 1860s bicycle. He waves to us while pedalling. Hockey teams or whole families ride on decorated wagons pulled by a tractor, and local business owners wave to us from their floats.

After the parade ends, we head for the fairgrounds and midway. The smells of caramel corn and cotton candy tease us as we approach. We hear the tunes from the merry-go-round, smell the horses, as dressage riders canter around a ring, and we see the riders line up for their jumps. We wait to ride the Ferris wheel, merry-go-round, flying swings, or other spinning rides, though the Ferris wheel ride and flying swings are less tempting to me for their height and speed. We walk up and down past hawkers, who try to persuade us to part with our coins in exchange for a chance to try the fishing game or throw darts at balloons on a backboard to win a prize. We have a little money to spend at the fair, but not enough to try everything, so we choose carefully.

The smell of hot dogs and sausages in the midway makes us hungry. We buy a hot dog or sausage on a bun from the hockey team or Junior Farmers booth outdoors, but we're also looking forward to our supper at the Evangelical United Brethren church booth inside the arena, so we're careful not to have too much now. We go into the arena to see if our exhibits have won any prizes and in the hopes of meeting any friends we might have missed on the midway. We see school and neighbourhood friends and go on rides with them, if we have any ride tickets left.

We make one last stop at the midway after supper, and Dad buys a bag of caramel corn for us to share on the way home. The sweet taste of the caramel corn is a perfect ending to an exciting day. We trade stories on the way home of prizes won, who we saw and what rides we went on. We help with evening chores, our minds filled with the colours and sounds of the fair, and as we settle into our beds that night, we are exhausted but still reliving those moments that we will wait another year to experience again.

A continuing tradition

We live in the city now, but we have almost always attended the fair. As recorded in *Fact and Fantasy: A History of Tavistock*, "Many former residents make it a home-coming."[12] That is certainly true for many who attend.

Our daughters have looked forward to the yearly day at the fair and enjoyed the parade, the midway rides and games. They have not only watched the parade but also participated in it. One year, our youngest daughter dressed as a gymnast and did cartwheels the whole parade route. As a result, she won a ribbon that she wore proudly.

We have brought friends, who have little to no connection with the village, to experience our home-town agricultural fair, and they've gone with us again and again.

Now that our children have grown, we still attend. Over the years, I have participated as both exhibitor and judge. Rides no longer take precedence. We go because it's our home-town community; we go to see friends and relatives, to see who has won the quilt contest, the knitting prizes, the art and the handicrafts. We go because we enjoy it.

---

[12] - Karl Seltzer, ed., Fact and Fantasy (Tavistock: Rotary Club, 1967), 107

Federated Women's Institutes and 4-H Girls' Clubs

When I was a young girl, my mother was a member of the Women's Institute (WI). She attended meetings once a month, except in summer, when all farm wives were busy with harvest and canning. My sister, Mary, and I attended a meeting or two with her. We were the entertainment, having been volunteered by our mother to play a duet on the piano in the hosting woman's home. It really was special since we got to dress up and perform pieces we had learned in our lessons.

The meeting, held on a week night, was opened and the business attended to first, and as we sat and waited our turn, I studied the woman's décor. I don't remember a thing about what the women discussed, since their concerns and projects were beyond me at the tender age of nine or ten. Meetings always concluded with a social time that included tea and coffee, plus some baked goods like pie or squares. We enjoyed the refreshments until Mom took us home, since we had school the next day.

I knew little about what the Institute stood for. It had to be something worthwhile, for on the door of our refrigerator was the picture of a Korean child whom the Anna P. Lewis WI sponsored for a time. Perhaps it was also a reminder for us to count our blessings that we had enough money for clothing, food, shelter and the opportunity to go to school, something this child could not do without our help.

The Anna P. Lewis WI planned a barbecue each summer, as a

social gathering that included their families. I remember attending one such event, but had forgotten that Uncle George, my Dad's older brother, was the one who lit the charcoal barbecue and roasted the wieners and sausages on the grill, while his wife Lenore, another active WI member, helped to distribute the grilled meat and buns when the barbecuing was done.

The 4-H Homemaking club was one of the Institute projects; that I knew. My sisters and I benefitted from those club experiences, and I cannot say that I liked one project over another. I was learning to sew and cook, doing it with fellow club members and enjoying myself, most of the time. Beyond the 4-H club, I still had no concept of the scope of Women's Institute projects.

It was in the writing of this book, as I recalled our 4-H activities, that I thought to research the origins of the 4-H club and the Women's Institute, our sponsoring body. I delved deeper into its history and purpose, and though this information is less personal to me, I feel its history ought to be at least mentioned. What follows is a brief overview of how both the Women's Institutes, including the Anna P. Lewis WI, and our 4-H Homemaking Club came into being.

Founding of the Federated Women's Institutes of Ontario (FWIO)

The Federated Women's Institutes came about through a sad sequence of events. Adelaide Hoodless, a rural woman, lost her 14-month-old son to a bacterial illness. Wanting to bring a positive outcome to her family's trauma, she strove to learn from the tragedy and to help other women to prevent another such painful experience. She learned about pasteurization—a method of destroying bacteria in raw milk—and discovered that had she boiled the milk she gave to her son, he would probably not have become sick and died.

Hoodless started spreading the word. She became interested in the Young Women's Christian Association (YWCA) in an effort to teach young girls skills in household management.

After a meeting in her home with Dr. Harrison, a professor of Bacteriology at the Ontario Agricultural College, she was invited to speak to members of the Farmers' Institute, an almost entirely male audience. She pointed out that "men were more concerned about the health of their animals than about the health of their children and that they fed their pigs and cattle more scientifically than they fed their families."[13]

Her speech so impressed a young farmer, Erland Lee, secretary of the Farmers' Institute, that he invited Hoodless to speak to a group of women in his home near Stoney Creek, Ontario. He and his wife Janet were aware of poorly educated rural women in their community and wished to create an educational organization to reach them.

Out of that meeting on February 19, 1897, the Federated Women's Institute was born. The stated goals included improving the quality of life for its members and their families, discovering

---

[13] - Federated Women's Institutes of Ontario, Ontario Women's Institute Story, 6

talents and improving speaking and leadership skills, promoting advocacy on a wide variety of issues that would make their homes, community and country a better place to live. Areas of concern were home efficiency; sanitation; household architecture; economic and hygienic value of food, clothing and fuel; a more scientifically based knowledge of raising children; health and morals of the people; and any other issues that might contribute to the betterment of the home. The movement to establish groups across the province flourished.

Anna P. Lewis Women's Institute is chartered

Mrs. Edmund (Laura) Hansuld, a resident of East Zorra Township, was interested in establishing an Institute in her area. She invited women of the community to her home for an initial meeting. Fifteen of the eighteen women who attended that inaugural meeting on December 3, 1946, became charter members. It was suggested to name the Institute after Miss Anna P. Lewis, daughter of a Women's Institute member, who was a home economist and the Director of Women's Institutes with the Department of Agriculture.

#

On the occasion of the 50th anniversary of the Federated Women's Institutes and the ninth anniversary of the Anna P. Lewis group, Mrs. Hansuld invited Miss Anna P. Lewis to attend their meeting. That evening Miss Lewis was named the honorary president of the organization that bore her name.

My grandmother, Flora, was also a member, as were my mother and several of my aunts. In fact, most women of the community joined the organization at some time.

Aside from attending Institute family functions with my mother or playing piano for a meeting, I was unaware of the purpose, the projects, and what the group had accomplished, except for the Girl's Club, of which I was a member.

The Anna P. Lewis Women's Institute has long been involved with youth education. Before the girl's club as I knew it, Mrs. Hansuld and fellow members established earlier groups: The Marigold Girl's Club, Marigold and Cabbage Club, Gladioli and Tomato Club. Those earlier clubs had specific goals in mind, but the greater purpose was to teach young girls about sewing, cooking, as well as taking care of the home and garden.

#

The Anna P. Lewis Women's Institute is one of ten Institute groups in Oxford County who organized Girl's clubs, also known as 4-H Homemaking clubs.[14] Institutes were also involved in establishing the Junior Farmers organization for young adults.

---

[14] - 4-H is a club for young people growing up in the country. The four Hs stand for Head, Heart, Hands and Health and are part of a pledge we repeated at each meeting.

#

The Anna P. Lewis Women's Institute is an affiliate of the Federated Women's Institutes of Ontario (FWIO), and also of the Federated Women's Institutes of Canada (FWIC). Both the FWIO and the FWIC are member organizations of the Associate Women of the World (ACWW).

Not all groups bear the name of Institute, but they are united under the common goal of working for the betterment of themselves, their families, their community and their country. Both Women's Institutes and 4-H Homemaking Clubs originated under the jurisdiction of the Department of Agriculture and its extension branch of Home Economics.

Anna P. Lewis Women's Institute begins a Homemaking Club

I received a phone call one day. Would I consider joining a group of girls for a 4-H Homemaking Club? I was excited and said that I wanted to join. I had just turned thirteen and was eligible, the absolute youngest age being 12 years of age, meaning that my sister Mary, who would be 12 in July, would need to wait until fall to join.

The first club that Anna P. Lewis would sponsor would be a garden club, and though it was a very big undertaking for a thirteen year old, my parents assured me they would help in every way possible. My mother, pregnant at the time, was probably relieved that she'd have help with the garden that year.

Our club meetings

We started each meeting by reciting the 4-H Pledge, in which we promised to use our head, heart, hands and health for the betterment of our world, much as the Women's Institutes started their meetings with the Mary Stewart Collect, a form of prayer about their purpose.

We would also grow familiar with the 4-H emblem which consists of 4 Hs, representing Head, Heart, Hands and Health, arranged into a clover-leaf style crest that was on the cover of each participant's manual.

#

Our 4-H leaders were women from the Anna P. Lewis Women's Institute, women who were willing to learn new skills or were already proficient in the selected unit. Sometimes leaders were women with daughters of their own, who were old enough to participate in the club. And, while the leadership was provided by women in the community, achievement was recognized by the Ontario Department of Agriculture and Food and its Home Economics extension branch. Home Economists from the department signed and handed out certificates we received on Achievement Days.

#

It would be hard to choose which leaders I appreciated most, for all of the women who led were competent and arrived well prepared. They were friendly and approachable and some of them were our neighbours. Among the leaders, we had several teams who worked exceptionally well together. Among these were Kathleen and Velma; my aunt, Doris, and her sister-in-law Dora; Shirley and Marie, daughter-in-law of Kathleen; and others. My mother assisted with a sewing unit, and Aunt Doris, with a cooking and entertaining project.

Each unit included hands-on work and note-taking. We covered a variety of topics and areas in homemaking. We learned about cooking (some units included: Meat in the Menu, The Supper Club, The Milky Way), gardening (4-H Home Garden)[15], entertaining (The Club Girl Entertains), sewing (Working with Wool, Cottons May Be Smart, Sleeping Garments), first aid (The Club Girl Stands on Guard), personal dress and grooming (Being Well Dressed and Well Groomed, Accent on Accessories) and needlework (Needlecraft).

Achievement Day

At the end of each unit, we attended an Achievement Day—a whole Saturday when we met with other girls and leaders from the same county. Coming from the community at large, I often knew girls from other clubs through school or community events. Aunt

---

[15] - See "Garden Club" - *p. 130*

Edith, my father's older sister, also taught a club unit when her daughter was involved and attended Achievement Day with her Girl's club.

Much preparation went into that day. If it was a sewing project, we displayed the garment or item we had made, as well as our workbooks, in which we recorded our accomplishments each week. Our workbooks also had instructions on topics such as sewing a facing, or proper hemming and finishing techniques. In a cooking club, we had recipes to try out at club meetings and at home.

For Achievement Day, each club was responsible for entering an exhibit, a demonstration, or a skit that showed what we had learned. The exhibit showed our club name and the sponsoring Women's Institute group as well as points we had learned over the six- to eight-week sessions, along with a sample project. The demonstration usually involved two or three girls showing a process and talking about it. The skit could be humorous or serious, and entertained while teaching.

Four items in a class were selected by someone in leadership, and all 4-H members were asked to judge those items on a small card. The card listed categories such as quality of work, suitability of materials and overall appearance. If it was a cooking unit, we might have been judging tea biscuits, and so we'd fill in the blanks. The card read "I place this class of 'tea biscuits' 3, 4, 1, and 2 for these reasons: … " There would be room for a few short notes on our reasons for placing the items in this order, then the last line read, "I placed this class of tea biscuits in this order for this reason …" and we were to complete the judging and hand in our cards.

Judging taught us analytical thinking but also to value our work and its quality, which was a good thing. At the same time, I found that process challenging and sometimes fraught with anxiety, especially when one of those projects belonged to someone I knew, even if that girl would not see my final mark. It also meant that I worked very carefully on my project, in the event someday it would be mine that was chosen for judging by all my peers.

Attending 4-H was a valuable experience, enjoyable because of the small group and at times more satisfying than my home economics class in high school, where the teacher was farther removed from rural living. Our leaders were capable, knowledgeable and approachable, and often quite skilled. Our group was small enough that if we needed help, we got it.

We could earn a County Honours certificate by completing 6 units (or projects) and a Provincial Honours certificate for completing 12 projects. I understand that there were also higher levels of recognition for eighteen and twenty-four units. We could usually complete two projects per year, and since I had begun at age 13 when the Anna P. Lewis WI initiated the club, I completed 13 units by the time I finished my first year in college.

#

Each member completing the project successfully received a coffee spoon with the 4-H crest on its handle. Eventually, those spoons became a scarce commodity, and also a prized item, as they were no longer given.

4-H Clubs have changed

The Ontario 4-H crest, not to be confused with the US 4-H crest, has changed somewhat over the years, but the pledge and motto remain the same.

Where once the girls' and boys' club projects were delineated by gender, the boys to work with animals and learn about field crops and the girls to concentrate on homemaking skills, things have changed. Further adjustments have been made by 4-H Ontario when public schools announced they would no longer provide life skills training and closed down their home economics and family studies programs—all this at a time when boys were finally allowed into the kitchens and girls into the shops.

The 4-H organization saw a gap it could fill, for both boys and girls. The 4-H clubs are still largely based in rural areas but are open to anyone who wishes to participate and who pays the yearly fee, including youth from cities and towns. Along with traditional subjects, such as how to raise a calf or pig and show it at agricultural fairs, the projects range to personal growth, leadership, sports, crafts, energy conservation and environmental awareness. There's also a new venture into public speaking.

Both girls and boys, from 9 to 21 years of age (as well as a trial modified program for six year olds), can take whatever projects are being offered in their area for a yearly fee, payable to the local 4-H association, which in turn hands over most of the fees to 4-H Ontario. Whereas the Ministry of Agriculture once funded the 4-H program, now the 4-H program is run independently through fees, sponsors and donations.

Mary Lou Ross, a fellow Girl's club member of our area, has been a 4-H leader for many years, including the years her two daughters were involved. She still occasionally helps out, when a club requires an extra leader or an extra set of hands.

She has led during the transition from girls only in the homemaking club to projects including both boys and girls, and said, "Sometimes boys will not take a unit if it involves sewing."

#

She said that youth, who are 4-H members and are fifteen years of age or older, can assist adult leaders. Such members are called youth leaders and earn a credit for each accomplishment, one for the leadership component, and a second one as member of the club completing the project. All projects, including those locally approved, rely on material distributed through the 4-H Ontario website to approved leaders; members can download the material for the project they're taking. Subjects have included photography, drama, cooking, sewing, bread making, knitting, and projects on working with chocolate and learning about maple syrup.

"The emphasis is less on manuals and more hands-on," Ross says. This new emphasis is in line with the 4-H motto "Learn to do by doing." Ross mentioned a particular project called Walk on the Wild Side which covered the environment and nature and included an overnight camping trip. One of the locally approved projects that she taught was scrapbooking.

Ross says there is a continuous process within the 4-H organization to create and approve both new and current projects that would be of interest to members. With so much change since my membership days, I am curious to see how 4-H will further evolve.

Work of the Women's Institutes, then and now

The Federated Women's Institutes of Canada have been instrumental in bringing about many changes to school curriculum, laws and safety precautions. Mrs. Kathleen Bickle, a former elementary school teacher and a long-time active member of the Anna P. Lewis WI, explained that women in individual institute groups write up a resolution of issues that concern them. A representative takes this resolution to the district conference. If the resolution is passed by the district, the resolution goes on to the area conference. From the area, an advocacy representative takes it to government, which then considers the issues and passes motions to put them into effect. Often local MPPs were involved, however, the present advocacy coordinator, Judith Moses (at the time of this writing), believes that in putting matters forward to the Ministers is "more direct, more efficient and most importantly politically neutral."[16]

#

---

[16] -Federated Women's Institutes of Ontario, "Advocacy Update." *Home & Contry Rose Garden*, Spring and Summer (2009):11.

A concern at the time of this writing is the new Product of Canada labelling rules. Women's Institute (WI) members are being asked to act on it.

As a national group, the FWIC has been instrumental in bringing about many changes. Among them are such items as:
- establishing the MacDonald Institute at the University of Guelph,
- setting up a course in Household Science at MacDonald Institute,
- requiring pasteurization of milk,
- putting music and home economics on the school curriculum,
- having bread wrapped,
- labelling poison containers,
- painting white lines on the centre of provincial highways,
- labelling garments for quality,
- installing flashing lights on school buses,
- stopping for school bus flashing lights,
- legislating dimming lights for motorists meeting other cars on the road, and
- requiring breathalyzer and blood tests for motorists.

#

Individual organizations can participate in projects of the ACWW or FWIC and they can initiate projects in their own community. Mrs. Bickle mentioned projects that the Anna P. Lewis group had initiated and others to which they had contributed at the worldwide, national and community levels.

At the world-wide level, the Anna P. Lewis Women's Institute once sponsored Korean children until their group ran low in funds and could not continue. Another project at the international level was Pennies for Friendship that helped establish pumping stations for wells so that people in Africa would have fresh water for drinking and sanitation.

Community awards remain one of the group's favoured projects. Daughter of charter member, Elizabeth Wittig, Kathleen Bickle was my first and second-grade teacher before her marriage, and so education has been important to her. She said, "One of my favourite projects is the English proficiency award that we give to graduating Grade 8 students of both Hickson and Tavistock Elementary Schools each year."

Mrs. Bickle said, "We sponsor the Explorers Club, a Tavistock-based group as well."

The group has, from time to time, catered for weddings—including mine—and anniversary celebrations, and it has also worked with other Oxford County Institute groups when the International Ploughing Match was held in the county, and the Institutes, as a group, did the catering. Aside from those occasional events, the organization plays more of an educational role for rural women than a fundraising organization. In fact, the primary goal of the Institute, as established by its founder Adelaide Hoodless, was to educate rural women, many of whom would have had limited schooling with no access to post-secondary education.

The Anna P. Lewis Institute is also active in the Fall Fairs each year and sponsors a competitor in the Fall Fair Ambassador contest each year. The group also presents the Laura Hansuld Trophy to the Junior competitor in the Fall Fair competition with the most points for entries.

In the adult department, they sponsor prizes for two categories in honour and memory of long-time members: the Anna McKay Special, for an item made with a granny square,[17] and one for my aunt Doris, the Doris Steinacker Memorial Special, for humorous short poetry.

#

This group also invites speakers to meetings that are open to the community. An area man spoke at one of these meetings. He had been treated at an area hospital, after suffering extensive burns to his body in an accident. The women, impressed by the man's story and the work doctors and nurses had done to help him, made donations to the burn units of hospitals in the district.

#

At one time, most women in the community were members of the Women's Institute, but fewer new members come on board now as more women work away from home. Still, the long-time

---

[17] - See "Granny Square" - *p. 154*

members continue their programs. Institutes have done much for their community both individually and as a whole, and yet they see changes afoot in the organization. Once meetings were most often held in daytime hours, but to accommodate women who work outside the home, they now hold meetings in the evenings. Seniors who would not otherwise get out might ride with younger members.

For my part, I am grateful to the women for sponsoring our girl's club, providing the woman power to lead the groups, and for all the learning I gained there. I think I speak for others in the community who also have benefitted from their dedication. For all they have done, a hearty thank you.

Part III
Growing Up

Bush Walk

Rubber booted
we follow the furrow of tumbled soil
to the woodlot.

Branching arms of stately elm, maple and beech
canopy the forest floor
pinholes of light touch the cool wet earth
stripe-suited jack-in-the-pulpit preaches
to scarlet trilliums, lacy fern, and velvet green moss

Lavish clumps of dogtooth violet hide in the shade—
a perfect bouquet

burdocks, those hitchhikers,
come home with us
warm fistfuls of wilting flowers and rosy cheeked smiles
on Mother's Day.

Trip to the Woodlot

In early May on a Sunday afternoon, my sisters, Mary and Bonnie, and I put on our rubber boots, sweaters and jackets for our walk with Dad to the woodlot at the back of our farm. It's cool yet, and the ground will be wet under the trees. Our little sister stays with Mom; in a few years, Joan will be old enough to take this walk too.

The woodlot is a stand of trees—spruce, elm, maple, and beech—at the back of our farm, the place where Dad cuts our Christmas trees every year, and where my father and grandfather would have cut firewood for their stove. This is also the place where we learn about wild flowers.

We walk across the yard, past the orchard, and along the furrows in the ploughed field. The clay soil is softening, warming with the sun, and the ridges shift under our feet, making the walk slow. We stay off the field when the ground is wet. We girls have tried that, against Mom's better judgment, and so we know our boots get stuck in the gooey mud.

Our dog follows us there; he goes everywhere we go. He runs ahead, barks, waits, then runs back to us again and again in the time it takes us to cross the furrows. Before we make it to the bush, Dad turns, puts his finger to his lips and says, "Shh." And he points to the white-tailed deer at the edge of the trees.

When we finally reach the bush, we watch for the burdocks on the plants. Burdocks are prickly balls of plant material that grow on tall bushy stems, and if we brush by the plants, the burdocks stick to our sweaters, our socks—anything soft that they come in contact with.

We look up, way up, to the tops of the tall trees to see the sky, and we see how the light shines down around the leafy treetops. We look down to see the pattern that the sun's rays make on the ground and the shadows that the trees make. We smell the dampness in that space.

We learn the names of trees right here, for Dad knows them all. Beechnuts lay on the ground and we gather a few to peel and eat. The nuts are bland, like peanuts before roasting and salting, but they are crunchy.

#

Dad shows us the moss growing on the bark of fallen trees and on stones. It is soft and cool and feels like velvet. Clumps of ferns with lacy edges grow here too, along with Mayapples, plants that look more like leafy umbrellas. By this time, the trilliums are blooming, red and white flowers that we dare not pick. I wonder who named the Jack-in-the-pulpit. The plant looks like a little man with a green striped suit standing in a pulpit, like the one our minister stands in to deliver his sermon. God surely has a good sense of humour, making such a plant.

We go as far as we can, closer to the fence line, but we stop just before the small pond and look for hoof prints where the deer passed through. The fence line marks the border of our land and our neighbour's land, Dad says, and each owner has a small lot of trees like ours, all nestled together.

#

A multitude of dogtooth violets growing in the shade reward us for waiting. The plants have tiny yellow flowers on fine green stems, and are not really violets but lilies. We each pick a handful to take back to our mother.

Our trip back to the house seems shorter than the trip out. We have things to talk about, and our flowers to deliver.

We present those now-wilting flowers from our hot little hands to Mom, who fills a small glass with water and places our flowers in it.

Our last task before taking off our coats and boots is pulling the burdocks from our clothing and from the dog's coat. It takes time; the burdocks are prickly and our dog's winter coat is long.

The yellow violets, whose earthy aroma I associate with spring, and of course, the occasional missed burdock, are fleeting souvenirs of our springtime trip to the woodlot.

Sunday Mornings

Shoes shining like new pennies
starched dress that defied wrinkles
skin scrubbed and hair curled
I was admonished to behave

Sitting on our little painted chairs
              lined up in a perfect row
we sang songs of praise
prayed our simple prayers
and listened to stories of people
who were just as silly as we are

and, oh, how hard it was to sit still

Sunday Drives

Sunday afternoons
we pile into the Chevy
      cruise down country roads
         with the knock knock of gravel hitting metal
        and tires humming on pavement

golden wheat and tall corn stalks catch Dad's eye
he points to barley flattened by wind and rain
      tells us to watch for horses

hush, mother says to her sardine-packed children
      in the back seat

yellow mustard decorates green fields
black-clad Mennonites ride in buggies
      behind trotting horses
 we cheer dogs running alongside us
 and watch them turn away   at some imaginary line

are we there yet?

and we see where Dad is headed

A Nickel to Spend

Shirts, handkerchiefs, towels and sun hats,
parasols and fly swatters;
everything that parents buy

I see gumballs, licorice,
ice cream and candy

indecision is bigger
than the nickel in my pocket

Once Upon a Sandbox

its painted boards once leaned against
the silver birch
that shaded hatless children

sand turned to muck with hose and bucket
we built roads and riverbeds, fields and lanes
tractors planted and trucks got stuck

we drove those roads at five and seven
with tiny wheels and hoots of laughter
played out life with sand and water

Attic Playhouse

Under the roof is a playhouse
    with its familiar odour of heat and yesterday
leather skates lean against each other
      like fallen dominoes
        March through December

outgrown Sunday shoes wait for the next pair of feet
castoff clothes crammed in a crumbling cardboard box
yellowed notebooks—lined with ancient scribbles

crank the gramophone
        inside its heat-blistered black box

it warbles a tune
in symphony with buzzing flies
      hypnotized by the light of one window
      and too dazed to find another exit

C. R. Wilker

Pencils, Lunchboxes and Compositions

It might have been the row of new backpacks and lunchboxes that sparked the reverie. Or maybe children and teachers anticipating their return to school. Whatever started it, I pictured myself as I was years ago, arriving at my one-room schoolhouse, lunch box in hand.

#

My teacher steps outside the red-brick schoolhouse and rings the hand bell. Inside the school, she greets each of us with a smile and directs us to our desks, lined up in rows, bumper to bumper, facing the blackboard: small desks for the little kids, to gradually bigger ones for the older students, all in one large room. The board is already filled with sums and words and explorer's maps. Someone is sharpening a pencil and another opens his ink well and dips a pen into it, then writes something in a notebook.

At the beginning of every school day, we stand at attention to sing God Save the Queen, recite the Pledge of Allegiance and pray The Lord's Prayer.

As surely as autumn follows summer, we are in for our infamous first assignment of the year. It's to be a composition: "What I did on my summer vacation."

I know I didn't write one the first year. I still had to learn to read and write, excuse me, print.

In my mind, summers on a farm paled next to my grandparents' train trip through the Rocky Mountains or their winters in Florida. Their coffee table books intrigued me. There was more of the world to see, much more.

Just what does the teacher want to hear about? I tap my pencil on the desk and contemplate the task, discarding one idea after another.

I imagine my teacher yawning. Every child in our classroom—except perhaps Hartman, the boy in the wheelchair—had ridden on a tractor, picked beans from the garden and hoed rows of turnips that stretched for what felt like miles. Few of us travelled far from our hometown during harvest season.

At least once, I wrote about our trip to Ipperwash every August 1st weekend, when we ate picnic lunches on the beach, splashed in the lake and built sandcastles with our friends. The day always ended too soon.

I don't remember if I wrote about the new batch of kittens we found in the barn, and how we had to search for them again the next day. Sometimes we watched from a distance as the mother cat picked up her babies by the scruff of the neck and carried them to a new hiding place between bales of hay.

I might have described the grasshoppers that jumped from row to row of felled grain stalks after the harvester passed through the field and how we tried to collect them in jars, only to release them later. Or that we climbed apple trees for other reasons than picking fruit. Then there was the year we retired the old outhouse, with its remnants of Eaton's catalogues, to the bonfire. What a big fire that made.

I doubt that I told my teacher about the seemingly endless job of podding peas, bushels of them, in the shade of the walnut trees while Grandma told us stories, and how glad we were to see the last bushel emptied. I wouldn't have written about the shelves lined with canning jars in our cold cellar after days of steam-filled kitchens, the sweetness of strawberries, raspberries and peaches, or the tangy aroma of pickled beans, cucumbers and beets, food that would fill our stomachs during the winter.

I was only seven, eight, nine, 10 or 11, sitting in a gradually bigger desk in that red-brick schoolhouse. All those activities were as ordinary as brushing my teeth three times a day.

If I wrote about camping in our makeshift blanket tent between those tall walnut trees, I would have to confess that we often ran into the house by midnight, frightened by night noises or startled by our dog or cat squeezing in between us.

I wonder how many times the teacher heard about gathering twigs and dead wood from the orchard for a wiener roast. Our grand finale was roasting marshmallows, burning them to black and sliding the whole gooey mess off the pointed sticks and into our mouths.

#

College and motherhood have come between then and now and another school year is about to begin. With three daughters on their own, we have no students in either elementary or high school. Their schools and even my own later experience in high school—with so many more students per class—have been so different from my one-room schoolhouse. I wonder, do teachers still ask what their students did on summer vacation?

Dream Pages

Adults talk of wheat and barley and market prices
but I turn the pages of grandma's photo album
and hear the clickety-clack of steel wheels on tracks

I chug through mountains
eating wild antelope and Brussels sprouts
and meet people who cross the country
because they can

chin on the window ledge
I watch curly-horned sheep whiz by
they dine on pastures bigger than any I've seen
    —do they wonder at the monster that rushes by?
lakes nestle between folds of land
and mountains wear white hats even in summer

after hundreds of miles we stop
 "all aboard" the conductor calls
the locomotive's sooty breath
drifts through the open window

the train picks up speed
passengers sidestep their way to a seat
talking with accented syllables

I ask where they come from
and where they are going

and only return
when my grandmother offers lemonade.

School Days

Blackboards
painted with white words
numerals to add and subtract
green and blue geography lessons

we   loyal subjects of the Queen
       whose royal splendour
         supervises from her frame on the wall

we sing God save her
reciting the prayer
       forgive others
       who trespass against us
the small to the tall
mutter to God   whose face we cannot see

at our desks
 indented by inkwells
 and pencil slots
we open our minds
to adventurers and far off places
inking our brains
 with new words strange ideas
sorting chaos into order

at the swing of the hand bell
restless bodies
spring from confined spaces
brains and bodies replenish
from tin lunch boxes and thermos bottles

the schoolyard beckons
ropes beat a rhythm with our skipping feet
    Teddybear   teddybear   say goodnight
    Teddybear   teddybear   turn out the light

the crack of a bat and the runner's off
    running running
      the wind blows our hair

until the bell   ringing
calls us back to the classroom

The Music Lesson

The teacher tells us
about half notes   quarter notes
rests and tempo

In my bumper-to-bumper desk fit tight to yours
we beat out patterns on aging wood
our feet barely touching the floor

 Treble clef
       the lacy clef that our mothers sing
bass   the big "C"
       our daddies sing

 Andantino
it's dancing music
legato
and I whisper "slowly now"

The teacher's fingers
dance across the blacks and whites

An octave would be too much
for your small hands
even mine barely make it

My Amish Friends

Old Order Mennonites from Ontario and Pennsylvania bought neighbours' farms, pulled out hydro lines and settled in with their families. Their horses, buggies, and granny wagons populated our county roads and travelled at a leisurely pace.

The women wore long, solid-coloured dresses, of a similar style, in bright pinks, blues and greens, and they wore their hair braided and tucked under organdie prayer caps. The men, with their similar haircuts and bushy beards, wore plain shirts and black pants. The boys wore black-brimmed hats like their fathers, and in summer wore lighter straw hats. At all times, the children were dressed as diminutive adults.

The Hertzlers and Smokers were related to each other. We had two Davids in our school. To tell them apart, the teacher called them David A. and David B. David A. wore dark-rimmed glasses and had straight black hair, while David B. had light brown hair and freckles on his nose, like his sister Lydia. The girls were Lydia, Rachel, and Barbara. They walked to school together from the west, a little farther than the quarter mile that my sisters and I walked. Barbara, Rachel and David A. lived on the 10th line, while Lydia and David B. lived on the side road.

The Amish children stood apart at first, sticking together and watching, but not for long. They were like us; they loved to run and play, so they soon joined in the schoolyard games of tag and baseball. The girls skipped with us. They all spoke excellent English, teased and joked as we did, and soon we got along and worked together. Sometimes, though, they talked amongst themselves in German, when they had a secret to share. That was when I wished I knew German—the Pennsylvania Dutch dialect they spoke, that I would learn later was a part of my mother's ancestry.

Watching them play, I held in questions at school that I'd ask Mom at home. "Why do the girls wear long dresses? Why is their hair braided under those white caps? Why do they wear black stockings in summer? Why do the boys have the same haircut? Why? Why? Why?"

Mom answered, "Hush, we cannot ask."

In spite of our differences, Lydia became my friend. She was the same height and age as me, and for once I had a girl in my grade instead of just boys. Lydia had twinkling blue-green eyes and a round, serious face, but she could be funny too. I felt less sure of her cousin Barbara.

Barbara, fair-haired and the tallest of the Amish girls, was always so quiet when we played together. She'd look at me and whisper in Lydia's ear when I was nearby, or talk with Lydia in German so I would not know what she was saying. I wanted to cry when she did that. Did she not like my dress? Was she jealous that Lydia was my friend? What had I done to make her mad? I decided that she just did not like me.

Except for some initial shyness, the Amish children were cooperative and well behaved. They read as well as we did and caught on quickly to new work. They worked hard at whatever they did.

The teacher had made a health chart, wrote everyone's names

on it and hung the chart in the classroom. Every day, she'd ask us if we washed our hands, brushed our hair and our teeth, how many hours of sleep we had last night. We got a star on the chart every time we had done something to take care of ourselves.

On a particular morning, the teacher had asked, "Did you sleep eight hours last night?"

David A., who was usually very cheerful, suddenly looked anxious. He put up his hand and answered, "I had to get up early to do my chores."

It worked out to only ten minutes less than the eight hours. The teacher smiled and said, "That's close enough, David." Then David relaxed and smiled too.

On the last day of the school year, we were outdoors playing Red Rover and other group games. Afterwards, we sat in a circle on the grass, waiting for our next instructions. The teacher held up her camera to take a picture of her students, and the Amish children put their heads down, the older ones reminding their younger siblings to do the same so their faces would not be seen.

I asked about that at home too. Something was said about photographs being "graven images," but I still couldn't see what was bad about photos.

Changes were coming, and the school board made decisions on our behalf. The one-room schoolhouses in our county would eventually close. We were bused to other schools for Grades 6, 7, and 8. Lydia, Barbara, David A. and David B. rode on the school bus to the next school. Lydia sat with me on the bus many of those days, which didn't go over well with Barbara.

At the end of Grade 8, we went on a school trip to Niagara Falls. The Amish children were allowed to go too, as this was an educational trip. I remember walking across the grounds at the Brock Memorial Tower at Queenston Heights, Lydia in her long dress, with black stockings and shoes, and me in a shorter dress, and shoes and socks. We had our lunch bags in hand, and I also had my camera, a gift from my uncle Jack.

My shoelace had come untied. The ground was damp under the trees, and wanting to take good care of my camera, I handed both my camera and lunch bag to Lydia. Suddenly conscious of what that might mean to her, I asked, "Are you allowed to hold it?" She nodded and grinned, her eyes sparkling in her friendly way, and I bent to tie my shoelace. I collected my things and we headed for the school bus and the long ride home.

I went on to high school, but Lydia did not. The Amish children stop at Grade 8 and get the rest of their education at home. The girls learn to cook, bake, can, sew, and look after younger children. The boys help their fathers with the ploughing, seeding and taking care of the cattle, horses and chickens. And they get married young.

#

One June day, when I was still in school, Lydia drove their family's horse and buggy to our farm and delivered strawberries that my mother had ordered. She gave my mother a note for me. They would be moving back to Pennsylvania and she wanted to keep our friendship going. She had written her new address on it so that I might write to her.

We wrote back and forth for some months, but our lives were so different. She was far away and getting married while I planned to study to be a teacher. We were living our separate lives, with the future before us, hers to have children soon, and mine to finish high school and go on to college.

Before we stopped writing, I received a special piece of news in a letter from Lydia. She had allowed her cousin Barbara to read my letters. She hoped that was okay with me. Then she told me that Barbara wanted to be my friend too. Barbara and I each wrote a letter before our letter writing stopped, but it was good to know that we could be friends in spite of our differences. Those letters are long gone, but the warm feeling remains. I'm glad that Barbara and I were able to connect.

If it were possible, I would love to see Lydia again, and I think, even in all the time that's passed since those one-room school days, that we're still kindred spirits.

Good Cooks

I shall always associate good food with my mother. Her mother was a good cook who taught her daughters everything she knew. Grandma Ardena showed them the importance of using fresh garden vegetables, and meat from the butcher shop or the family farm. She also taught them how to bake.

My mother loves to cook and bake. She never tires of trying new recipes. She makes barbecued chicken that puts the phrase "finger-licking good" into a whole different category than the franchise that makes the same boast, and her baked beans are the best I've ever tasted. At extended family gatherings, she's known for her superb raspberry pies.

Mom told me once of her dream to one day open a little bakery or tea room. That hasn't happened, but she has had opportunities to cook and serve large numbers of people when she worked for a woman named Ruby in her catering business, and on other occasions when she has entertained and served people. Later she worked for Ruby's grandson Bill, who opened a restaurant in town. There Mom worked on the salad bar and also made 75 pies on Saturdays—more pies than I'd ever want to see in one day.

#

Just as my mother learned from her mother, my sisters and I tried our hands at cooking too. By working alongside her in the garden, we learned which peas were ready for picking, which cucumbers made the best pickles and which ones were suitable only for relish.

"Start with good ingredients," she would say, "and the product will be good."

We helped with cooking, canning, freezing, and of course, learned about food safety and cleaning up after ourselves. But the best part, after all the hard work, was sitting down to a delicious meal, with vegetables we had grown, preserves we had canned, or better still, a raspberry pie, still warm from my mother's oven.

Experiments in the Kitchen

When we were old enough to be useful in the kitchen, Mom assigned us each the duty of taking turns making lunch for the family. The choice of what we made was only limited by the ingredients we had on hand, which usually included our favourite foods. What is there to dislike about cooking when we could make what we liked to eat?

We knew what we were getting for lunch when it was Bonnie's turn—wieners and beans. All that had to be done was to heat some wieners in a pot of water, open a can and warm up the beans. The beans weren't at all like Mom's baked beans, but it was a whole lot faster. Besides, Bonnie was just learning to cook.

One year, we had purchased a sandwich maker for Mom for Mother's Day, to make the production of our favorite—grilled cheese sandwiches—a little easier for her. We were intrigued by the waffle plates that came with it.

Mary and Bonnie decided to try out the waffle-making capabilities. It seemed easy enough. They followed a recipe, mixed the batter, and plugged in the appliance, anticipating the waffles we'd have for dinner that evening.

I don't know what went wrong, and maybe they didn't either. The waffles were crispy on the outside and soft in the middle. A mushy mess. What we had for supper that evening, I don't remember, but the would-be waffle makers had a good deal of clean up afterwards. I'm not sure we ever mastered waffle making in our home. Dad teased the girls for a long time about the waffle mess. They blush at the reminder and wish he'd forget about it, but he doesn't, and they know he does it in fun, with a smile.

#

Mom put me in charge of dessert one evening. Next to making waffles, chocolate pudding seemed pretty easy.

As I measured the cocoa from the tin, I thought, *Mmm, if some chocolate is good, more must be better.*

The pudding smelled good as it cooked, and I restrained myself from tasting, lest there not be enough to go around. At dessert time, I dug my spoon into my pudding, waiting for the chocolatey taste to satisfy my craving, but I soon realized something was wrong. The others noticed it too.

Worried about a lecture over wasting good food, I admitted to adding extra cocoa powder. I don't remember if we added sugar to our pudding, ate it heroically or threw it out, but that was the day I learned that the recipe was just fine as it was.

Perfect Pie Crust

Mom always said that the trick to perfect pie crusts is in using lard, but also that the dough must be chilled before rolling it out. All along, I had thought that it was only the thinness of the crust that mattered, but Mom was an expert pie maker, and so I knew her word was good.

One hot summer day, when Mom was driving the tractor for harvest, I got my chance to make a pie. Mom had assigned me babysitting and cooking duties. Preparing supper included making dessert.

Mom often mixed pastry dough ahead of time and put it in the freezer. I was in luck. That morning, she had taken a ball of dough from the freezer, intending to make a pie later. I decided to surprise her and make a lemon meringue pie. My mouth watered just thinking of it. My three-year-old sister, Kim, played with her toys nearby while I rolled out the dough.

I rolled and rolled that crust until it was almost see through, and then set it carefully into the waiting pie pan. After trimming the excess dough, I frilled the edges just as Mom had taught me. The crust baked to perfection and I set it to cool, pleased with my efforts so far.

I must have misjudged my space, for when I had the filling cooked, cooled and ready to put in the shell, I accidentally hit the pie pan with the crust in it. The pan went crashing to the floor!

I had visions of serving the pie filling without the crust, but the crust survived amazingly well for its thinness. It only broke in two or three pieces. I picked up the shell and plate from the floor, put them back together and poured in the filling. Who would know besides me? My little sister had run into another room to get a toy and didn't see what happened, and therefore couldn't tell.

Everyone enjoyed my perfect pie.

The whole incident proved to me that rolling out a pie crust is a lot of work, let alone making it from scratch. Rather than compete with my mother and her sisters with their excellent pie crusts, I buy ready-made shells and only add the filling. And yet, nothing quite rivals the melt-on-the-tongue perfection of Mom's home-made pie crusts.

The Garden Club

I was thirteen years old and one of eight girls in a new 4-H club.[18] We were to plant a garden, with peas, corn, beans and cucumbers—all the vegetables we usually grew—and more, and we were to take care of it, too.

---

[18] - 4-H is a club for young people growing up in the country. The four Hs stand for Head, Heart, Hands and Health and are part of a pledge we repeated at each meeting.

My mother should have been celebrating, doing a little dance or something, because it would be me doing the bending and the planting, but she was pregnant with my little sister, who was due early in the summer, so both dancing and bending were out of the question.

The Women's Institute sponsored our club, which was intended to help the next generation of girls learn about homemaking.[19]

Our leaders, "green thumbs" themselves, handed out the garden kits at our first meeting. The packages were filled with smaller envelopes, labelled with the names of the vegetable and variety, even some flowers. We learned about soil preparation, planting and harvesting our crop. We also learned how to prepare the food and try it out with recipes from our club manuals.

It was an enormous project, but I wasn't entirely on my own. Dad helped me collect a soil sample for testing, and he cleaned up the garden with the tractor and scuffler, breaking up the soil and lifting out the weeds.

Mom helped me select a layout from my club manual that suited our garden plot. We measured the length of the rows and the spaces between them, marked the rows with small wooden stakes, and tied string to them, making long straight rows. We sorted the seed packets according to the rows, and only then opened the tiny envelopes one at a time.

---

[19] - 4-H Pledge: I pledge my head to clearer thinking, my heart to greater loyalty, my hands to larger service, and my health to better living for my club, my community and my country.

I knelt in the cool rich loam and planted thin, wispy carrot seeds, the same colour as the earth; radish seeds that were hard and rough; and small hard corn seeds that looked like the kernels that would grow on the cob. I covered the seeds with soil, using a hoe, then stood back to admire my work. I waited for the rain, hoped for sunshine, and watched the garden grow.

Dad tilled the garden from time to time, the tractor wheels running along each side of the row. The tractor had a kind of rake attached to it so that when he drove up and down the rows, it loosened the soil and lifted out weeds that grew between the rows. That meant I only had to hoe the rows and thin out the plants, but it was still a lot of work.

I pulled weeds, thinned the small seedlings, and hoed until my garden was clean. Too bad it never stays that way.

My weedless wonder almost made it into the 4-H magazine. One day a woman from the association came to check on my garden. My parents showed it to her, since I was away at a club meeting. The woman was impressed and wanted to take a picture of me in my garden. She said she'd come back later, but she never did. I missed my first photo shoot by a mere hour or two. I didn't realize how fortunate I was to have Dad's help until a fellow member told me of her constant struggle with weeds.

We had never grown kohlrabi and Swiss chard before, so I wasn't sure what to do with them. We tasted the kohlrabi and decided we liked it, but we didn't know what to do with Swiss chard, and so the plants just grew and grew and went to seed.

Marigolds and zinnias decorated the garden with their reds,

yellows, pinks and oranges, making it a cheerful place to work.

My baby sister came howling into the world in the middle of June, so Mom had to take time to rest up and tend her. Avid gardener that she is, she soon made short trips out to the garden to help pick vegetables for lunch and dinner.

Whatever we didn't eat from day to day, we processed and froze for winter. It was the first time I really cared about saving what grew in the garden—my garden.

Having a garden of my own was a rewarding experience. I learned about green, growing things, about soil and the care of plants and what to do with the produce afterwards. I still revel in spring, when the earth is renewed by rain. I like the feel of soil on my hands, the pleasure of watching my garden grow, and of tasting the eventual harvest.

Green Hands and Baskets Full of Cucumbers

I don't remember now whose idea it was to grow cucumbers. Was it was Mom and Dad's idea to start our college fund, or was it we three older kids who thought we'd get some spending money? What I do remember was an ad in a magazine about earning cash growing cucumbers—and the vast number of cucumbers we picked that summer.

#

I remember the picking more than the planting. The plants grew until we had vines spreading out over the ground, going every which way. Those rows stretched the length of the garden on the south side of the house, which was pretty long. When the blossoms turned into little cucumbers, we had to start picking. Every second day, rain or shine, we knew we had a job to do.

Mom and Dad showed us the chart the company gave us. The tiny cucumbers, about the length of my baby finger, were called gherkins and were most valuable. There were at least two sizes up from that, before we got to the big ones that were only good for making relish. Missing the little ones meant the cucumbers got bigger and bigger, and if we had a lot of rain, we soon had big fat cucumbers and many more little ones. A quarter acre of cucumber vines yields a lot of cucumbers.

We had to go searching for the little ones under the big leaves. It took so many more of them to fill a basket.

On harvest days, Mom sent us out to get started while she put our baby sister down for her nap. Mom left the window open so that when Kim woke up and called, we could hear her from the patch.

I would have been fourteen, Mary, 13, and Bonnie, 10. Joan was five and a little young to do the work, but she was a great help at carrying baskets. We'd call out her name and say, "Basket, please," and she came running with an empty basket, her curly blonde hair bobbing.

We picked when the sun shone, and we picked in the rain, because the plants kept on producing cucumbers, which grew and ripened. We sorted and bagged all those cucumbers at the end of every harvest day to be ready for the driver, who came out twice a week, every week, with his truck.

Handling all those cucumbers made our hands very green, especially when we picked during or after a rainfall. We greased our hands, then put on rubber gloves before we started, so the green would wash off more easily. Still, despite these precautions, some traces of the colour remained.

If we had an overnight stay at a friend's place or our aunt and uncle's, the deal was that we had to be home in time to pick cucumbers, and when we arrived home, we often had help. Aunt Doris pitched in more than once when she happened to be there.

We usually picked after lunch when my baby sister was sleeping, so Mom was free to help, but if there was a prediction for rain, we started earlier. And we sometimes worked in the rain too, with the mud sticking to our shoes, making them heavier and heavier as we moved along the length of each vine and from plant to plant. We picked as long as it took to gather all the cucumbers, until we covered the whole patch, a few hours for sure, depending upon how much help we had. Dad was always out there working with us, and he was the one who usually bagged the cucumbers when we were done each day. If other relatives or neighbours came by when we were picking, they came to the garden to find us and sometimes joined in as well.

Little creatures like the shaded part of the garden. One day when Mom parted the leaves to start picking, she saw a garter snake. Dad picked it out and tossed it far into the orchard.

"They're harmless," Dad said. But it made me nervous.

There were still cucumbers to be picked so I watched the ground very carefully, lest any more of them come slithering out. Bugs were okay, but I didn't like snakes at all. I had gloves on my hands, but still I didn't want to touch one or to be surprised.

#

Many bushels and bags later, we had picked hundreds of cucumbers. By the end of the summer, we were very glad to see the last of the truck. We added all the shipment totals that Mom was keeping track of and were pleased by the final amount. After Mom and Dad got their expenses, we each had a hundred dollars for our bank accounts—for our college fund rather than our pockets. It seemed like a lot of money at the time. We celebrated the end of cucumber picking by going out for ice-cream.

For a very long time afterwards, when I saw a jar of pickles at the grocery story, I'd remember our cucumber patch and all the picking we did. It may have paid well, but thinking back, I have to admit that I'm glad I didn't go in for any more market gardening.

What a Car!

A car pulled into the driveway, tires crunching in the snow that crisp January evening. Its headlamps lit up my bedroom window, but since I wasn't expecting any company, I continued what I was doing. I heard the car door close, and soon after the doorbell rang.

My landlady called upstairs and said that I had a visitor.

Who it could be?

There was Dad with a huge grin on his face, a sparkle in his blue eyes, and a set of keys in his hand.

I didn't expect to see my father that night—and much less did I expect him to be there with a car for me to test drive.

"I made a deal at Elliot's today," he said. "Thought you'd like to see it."

On the weekend, we had talked about the possibility of trading my trusty Corvair for another car, but I hadn't expected anything this soon.

"Want to go for a drive?"

Of course, I wanted to drive it! I ran up the stairs and pulled on my winter coat, taking a quick look out the window as I put it on. Under the reflection of my landlady's outdoor light was a '68 lemon yellow Camaro. Whooee!

I hurried down the stairs and out the door to where Dad waited, keys in hand.

I got in, readjusted the seat, rearview mirror, and side mirrors, and off we went for a drive around Waterloo.

"Do you like it? Is it a good fit?" he asked.

I agreed on both counts. I liked it very much.

When we returned to my landlady's home, we sat in the car and talked about how much it would cost, and how soon I could have it. One thing was for certain, I'd have to get a loan from the bank. Dad was willing to co-sign. All he needed was my approval and he could complete the deal. We would make the appointment at the bank the next week.

I had been driving the silver 1960 Corvair that once belonged to my grandfather Ted. My parents bought it from him when he decided to move to Florida to live. The Corvair had taken me safely and reliably to my weekend job at the nursing home during my last year of college, and then on the commute to Waterloo, where I boarded while working in a day care centre.

The Corvair was an experiment, with its engine in the back, and the trunk under the front hood. Ralph Nader had criticized General Motors soundly for it, but as it had been for my grandfather, the Corvair was a good little car that delivered a smooth ride. Its seat was just right for my short stature as it had been for my grandfather before me.

Grandpa Ted had always driven slowly down the freshly gravelled country roads so that the vehicle wouldn't get stone chipped; its body was still in excellent shape. Dad said that the car might run awhile yet, but sooner or later it would require some new parts and getting parts would be an issue, since the car was no longer being made. My favour, once set on the Corvair, was shifting rather quickly to the sporty Camaro, both for its appearance and for the practical reasons that Dad had explained.

The Camaro had just been traded in by a priest, who had purchased a brand new vehicle. The lack of stone chips on its shiny fenders and hood meant that the priest had treated the car with as much care as my grandfather had with the Corvair. The interior was clean and the upholstery looked like new. The Camaro was set low and the seat was easily adjusted. I felt like a queen behind the wheel, even if my bankbook didn't reveal a queen's pay.

Dad and Mom said they'd cover the down payment temporarily, but I'd have to pay it back by March, so they could buy fertilizer for spring planting. I'd also need new snow tires to navigate the country roads. I was getting poorer by the minute and I hadn't yet paid a cent for the car. Of course, I still wanted it. It was a dream car.

Dad drove the Camaro home that night and closed the deal the next day. I drove home for the weekend in my soon-to-be-retired Corvair, and Dad gave me lessons on changing tires, testing spark plugs, checking the oil level, and knowing when to add oil, as he had when I first drove the Corvair.

On Monday, after a trip to the bank, and an offer from the manager to work there instead, I left for the day care centre. When I drove into the parking lot, Penny, a fellow teacher, was out supervising children in the playground area. She whistled as I got out of the Camaro and approached the gate.

"Where's the fancy clothes to match the car?" she asked, with a cheerful grin.

I answered that I had spent it all on the car, and I had. I took good care of my lemon yellow Camaro, gave it regular maintenance, and far from the notion of cars being lemons, it proved reliable and took me many miles safely and in style.

It eventually needed a paint job, after someone backed into it in a parking lot at another day care centre. The driver had mistaken the Camaro for a snow bank on a dark winter morning. The supervisor, arriving in daylight, noticed the dent in my car. The parent admitted to his error and offered to pay for the repair and paint job, and I had it painted the same lemon yellow as before. The colour reminded me of sunshine—a particularly cheering sight on a gloomy day.

My future husband noticed me driving this car, so I suppose it was good for more than taking me places in style. We continued to drive the Camaro after he sold his fancy, gas-guzzling purple Swinger.

When our first child was born, she had to ride in her baby seat up front, since her car seat didn't work on the narrow back bench. About the same time, my car showed signs of rust, and so we agreed it needed to be patched and painted. I loved the lemon yellow and only grudgingly let my car be painted an electric blue. That wasn't as painful though as the white hood stripes and the wire trim that my husband said would suit it. He must have been missing his Swinger more than he let on.

We had barely brought the car home with its new paint job, when our neighbour, Larry, came across the street and offered to buy it. I was glad he liked it so much, because I didn't. Those white hood stripes and wire trim had turned my car into something foreign. We made the deal with our neighbour, and we went out that week and bought our first family car—a station wagon.

But I always remember the first real car that I bought with my own money: a sporty, lemon yellow Camaro that turned heads when I drove by.

Part III
The Wider Circle

Sam

Sam lived in a small house on a few acres at the corner of our field. When Dad was growing up, he visited Sam. Dad knew that Sam's collie was trained to protect his master, and one dared not enter without Sam there to restrain his dog.

Sam had worked as a stone mason for most of his life, a trade he had to give up when his hands trembled too much for the precise work he had to do. Besides, as the years went on, there was less call for stone masons. People started using concrete to build their foundations instead.

Sam often came to our home for coffee, and Mom took meals to him when he wasn't well. But it was a winter night that I remember most.

We were safe and warm inside our solid brick house as the wind whistled around the eaves and snow pounded against the windows. Hurricane Hazel had passed through the year before, breaking down trees, damaging homes, and ruining crops, so the weatherman's warning of a severe winter storm that night must have brought back the worry. My parents sat thinking of Sam, all alone in his drafty little house.

I remember Mom saying, "Harry, go and get Sam, bring him here for the night."

Dad drove over to Sam's place and did just that. Though I cannot remember much about him except for his whiskers, Mom said he liked seeing us little kids running around.

Sam had learned few of the social graces, or perhaps he didn't care much about them since he lived alone, but he took off his boots at Mom's request. She winced as he headed for the main floor bedroom, still wearing his outdoor hat and coat. He climbed into the clean, warm bed and was snoring within minutes.

Sam spent about six weeks in hospital the next year and died in the fall. Few family members remained, except for one relative in town who took care of Sam's last affairs—arranging his funeral and disposing of his few possessions. Sam's brother, also a bachelor, had died the year before. Beyond that were Sam's friends, Jack and Frank, who were close in age to Sam. My father and other younger neighbours were asked to be pall bearers. They carried Sam on his last journey to the cemetery.

After Sam's death, the relative in town claimed his property. Knowing that my parents wanted to purchase the land, the man sold it to them a few days later for twice the price it was worth, and because my parents had been promised the land, they bought it at the inflated price.

One day the next spring, my sister and I went with Dad to Sam's place. By that time, the house was a bare structure with front and back doors missing and spaces where the windows had been. My sister and I searched the stones and gravel for treasures, but found only a bent fork, grungy and mouldy. Not much of a treasure after all.

We climbed inside the house to take a look. The cook stove was gone, and there was a darkened square on the floor where the heater had been. If there had been any pictures on the wall before, I imagined a calendar from the grocery store or the feed mill in town, something to mark the days and months. Any furniture he had was gone too.

As my parents worked at dismantling the house and lean-to, where Sam kept his firewood, Dad found a china cup buried in the yard. They kept it to remember Sam.

Dad says he pushed at the house with the loader of the tractor, expecting the house to come down easily. He discovered that under the ship lath outer layer of Sam's house was a strong log structure. No wonder it wasn't coming down.

Sam's lot became part of our farm field, where Dad planted corn one year, and wheat or barley the next. Even now, when I look across the garden and the field beyond it, I can picture Sam's place and remember the quiet bearded man, in his dusty jacket and hat, walking across our kitchen floor in stocking feet, that night he slept over, so many years ago.

Just Like Daddy

When I was small
I tried to walk in Daddy's shoes
they were much too big for my small feet
I could not keep up with his long strides

Still, I cannot hold the pace
I try to match your steps, and fail

I strayed to bright objects
                        engaging sounds
and met with danger on the way

So, too, I am distracted from your purpose

and when I fell   or was afraid
I reached for Daddy's hand
his strong arms lifted me up
he comforted me

Just like that
you guide me back to the path
and remind me of your love

I'm still that small child
I wander

Anticipated Visits

When I was twelve years old, Grandma Flora and Grandpa Ted bought a lot on the side road close to the home farm where we lived, and where they had raised their children. The lot was graded and the foundation had been poured. I was looking forward to having my grandparents living close by. I wanted to spend more time with this grandmother I saw less often.

I must have been about seven or eight years old when I stayed overnight at their home in the city—a 30-minute drive from our place. Grandma understood about shadows in houses and left a nightlight on for me. She gave me choices and cooked the foods I liked to eat, and after the concert in the park, she and Grandpa treated me to ice cream. Grandma really listened when I talked to her; those pale blue eyes, like my Dad's, rested gently on me. She showed me that I mattered, even if I was only a kid.

I remember one of the dresses Mom made for me from fabric Grandma brought back from Florida. There was enough cloth for two dresses, back in the days when Mom dressed my sister and me alike.

During my grandmother's last weeks, my parents told us, "Grandma's really sick; she's going to the hospital," and "the doctors are going to operate." I would have liked to comfort her, except that I was ill too. Going to the hospital to see her was unthinkable since children were not allowed to go there as visitors, and even more so because I was recovering from whooping cough—though I was not nearly so sick as she. Being protected from hard truths, I never dreamed she wouldn't get better.

Grandma died during the operation. The cancer was advanced, and she was too weak to endure the trauma of surgery. All that was left to us kids was to prepare for her funeral and listen to the hushed tones of adult conversation and one-sided long distance calls to relatives.

Grandma lay there in her casket in her Sunday dress, hair curled and set. Her round, wire-rimmed glasses had been placed across the bridge of her nose where they normally sat, even if she didn't need them anymore. She would feel no more pain, my mother had said, as my Dad looked on, tears glistening in his eyes.

Grandma's funeral, on Valentine's Day that year, came in the middle of a winter storm. I was to stay at home, out of the cold wind that made me cough. The wind howled around the eaves like a pack of hungry wolves, increasing my sadness as I waited for my parents and sisters to come home. I tried to imagine the service that I was missing and remembered Mom saying that Grandma would be in heaven, a strange form of comfort, even to a child who believed in God.

#

Grandma never lived in that house. It was completed that spring and Grandpa moved in. His sister stayed with him for a time, taking care of the place and cooking meals.

But Grandpa didn't stay long in that house on the side road. Too many memories, I guess. I visited him wherever he went, even after he moved to Florida.

Our children have not known this set of grandparents, and I have missed sharing this part of my life with them. It's been a long wait, but on my next visit with my grandmother, I'll have so much to tell her.

Eggs Away

What happened that evening is an example of how determined my Grandpa Bill could be. My mother invited her parents and Jim, their boarder, to come to the farm for dinner. Jim had come to Canada from Holland with the intention of becoming a Canadian citizen and with plans to bring his fiancée as soon as he could afford it.

Grandpa had given up driving but had not yet sold his old green Studebaker. By this time, Jim had acquired his driver's license and had built up sufficient trust with my grandparents that Grandpa allowed him to drive it. So after Jim's shift at the factory, he drove to our home, bringing my grandparents along.

After dinner, we headed to Grandpa's car. We remembered his eight o'clock bedtime habit, though neither Jim nor Grandma were in a hurry to leave. Mom brought out a flat of fresh eggs from the hen house. Jim promptly set the eggs on the hood of the car and continued to talk.

Grandpa was agitated about getting home, and since he no longer drove, he started walking. One leg had been affected by polio when he was young and his limp had become more pronounced over the years, so he trudged along with his familiar rolling gait. Knowing his love of animals, my mother thought he had gone to see our pony that was tethered to a post in the lane eating grass. But Grandpa kept walking. I waited to see how far he would go before Jim noticed.

Jim's monologue halted mid-sentence when he saw my grandfather up the road and almost to the neighbour's fence post. A streak of unholy words shot from Jim's mouth, and he wasted no time depositing himself in the driver's seat. My grandmother was already in the front seat, waiting.

We stepped back from the car and watched in amazement as Jim hit the gas pedal and the car sped out the lane, gravel shooting from the back of his wheels, with the tray of eggs still on the hood. In all the excitement over Grandpa, we had forgotten about them.

Jim pulled up next to Grandpa and then rescued the eggs, while Grandpa folded his weary body into the back seat. I imagine Jim got the silent treatment all the way home. That was my Grandfather for you.

Kitchen Talk

While my grandmother and I made pancakes
she talked of home

starting with the sifting of flour into a bowl
continuing through the cracking of eggs
and measuring of milk

Fast as her spoon stirred
all this talk of sisters and hijinks
as if the ingredients had loosed her tongue

She was silent for a while
as if she had let out one too many secrets
in her kitchen spiced with sausage and sauerkraut
and geraniums flowering in summer windows

Poured batter into sizzling oil
watched the bubbles rise
and the stories build
faster than her homemade bread

Flipped over the cake, perfectly browned
added it to the steaming heap
Grandpa ready with his fork
maple syrup and butter waiting

And the stories stop here

Crochet Lessons

Grandma Ardena crocheted many pretty things for decorating her home. She made fancy trims to sew on the edge of pillowcases, and doilies that decorated end tables and hung over the backs and armrests of upholstered chairs. I noticed, too, that Grandma often brought her crocheting along with her wherever she went.

This was one thing I hadn't seen my mother do. One day, when I was about nine or ten years old, I watched Grandma crocheting a doily. I looked at the intricate design and said how pretty it was.

"Would you like to learn?" she asked.

"Yes." I wanted to try, even though it looked complicated.

Grandma pulled a hook and an extra ball of crochet cotton from her bag. She showed me how to hold the hook and thread, then put her hands on mine to help me get started. Making the first loop was easy, but pulling the hook through that tiny loop was much more difficult. I tried again and again, but the tremor in my one hand made it hard. I grew increasingly frustrated. Finally, I stopped and said I couldn't do it.

If Grandma was disappointed, she didn't show it. She continued with her tiny doily, and I decided, in those moments, that it was too hard. I would never try it again.

The Granny Square

After graduating from college, I taught in a city day care centre. Everywhere I went, I saw women wearing crocheted hats and scarves. I admired the poncho my co-worker wore that she'd crocheted with lush yarn of many colours.

Perhaps yarn would make it easier. I'd try again.

The local YMCA offered classes on everything from conversational Spanish to crafts and crocheting, so I signed up for crocheting. Bigger hook, thicker yarn, and a few lessons later, I was crocheting with ease. I enjoyed the sessions, with more credit to my classmate Ann, than to our instructor. Together we learned all the stitches we'd need for almost any project.

When I went home for the weekend, I told my mother that I wanted to make an afghan. First I'd need to learn how to crochet a granny square. I wondered if she might teach me.

"I can't help with that, but Anna could," Mom said. "She crochets a lot. She'd love that."

And so I called. Mrs. McKay was pleased, and we set a lesson date. I looked forward to our lesson with excitement and a touch of nervousness, for Mrs. McKay had been crocheting longer than I had been alive.

Her son greeted me at the door. "Mom's in the dining room. She's waiting for you."

I could see that this was occasion for tea and cookies and a social visit, not just a lesson.

She had put out her best tea service and china cups and saucers. She smiled, said hello, and indicated where I should sit.

Mrs. McKay was a tiny woman, with snow-white hair tied back in a tiny bun, bobby pins keeping all but a few stray hairs in place. Wire-rimmed glasses sat low across the bridge of her nose. Her eyes, pale with age, still sparkled and I sensed that she saw feelings I might try to hide. Her long dress reached to her ankles and her customary shawl would keep her warm in the old house. She walked slightly stooped, giving the impression of frailty.

I had been in the McKay home before. Even before Anna's husband died, Mom sent us the short distance up the road with fresh baked cookies or muffins. I enjoyed those breaks from chores as much as Anna did. But now Anna wasn't getting out of the house often, except for doctor's appointments, church, and Institute meetings. My mother knew she was lonely.

We drank strong tea from china cups at the polished dining room table. She asked about my job in the city and how I was doing. She always cared about the answer.

Evidences of her Scottish heritage, the tartan and Scotch thistle, decorated her dining room, and every afghan displayed in that room was made with granny squares. So many squares, so many colours. Joseph's coat of many colours couldn't have been brighter or more wonderfully made.

#

After tea, it was time for the lesson. She directed me, "First, crochet a three-chain string." Thinking she was going too fast for a beginner, she asked, "Do you know how to crochet a chain?"

I assured her I could do that. With my bulky yarn, and thick crochet hook in hand, I produced the required chain stitches, and then joined the stitches to make a circle as she instructed. Single stitches came next. Again she asked if I knew, and again I said yes. I crocheted while she watched, her hands always busy with her own work.

"My, you learn quickly."

I told her about my class at the YMCA.

I followed Anna's instructions and found the pattern predictable. It was easier and faster than I thought. Soon I had a small square that looked almost as good as hers. She was delighted with my progress.

"You'll get better with practice," she said.

Not wanting to overtire her, I excused myself and we said our goodbyes at the door. She thanked me for coming, and I, in turn, thanked her for the lesson.

#

Teaching me to sew granny squares together would be another woman's job. Anna's failing health dictated her move to a nursing home in town. When I visited her there, she seemed restless, as if something were missing. If seeing her without crochet hook in hand felt odd, making conversation was far more difficult. I left with a huge lump in my throat and tears threatening.

Anna died a month or so afterwards.

Impressions of that tiny woman live on each year at the local agricultural fair. The Women's Institute, of which Anna was a lifetime member, sponsors a special category in her name. It awards prize money for any craft article made from a granny square.

Whenever I see a granny square, I think of Anna.

Persistent Little Sister

Kim, my youngest sister, had five mothers—our mother and four big sisters. When she didn't get the desired response from one, she moved on to the next. There was no end to her motivation. She got what she wanted most of the time, and a spanking once in awhile. She was clever, and she learned what our soft spots were. She never gave up!

Having thirteen years between us meant that I missed a lot of her growing up years. I was teaching when she was in grade school, and raising my own young children when she was a teenager. No longer the pony-tailed youngster, but a young woman with a preschooler, she shared this story at Mom and Dad's 50th anniversary celebration—remembrances of her growing up years on the farm.

"Some of my earliest recollections are of me as a kid who didn't want to go to bed at night. There are a few sisters present today who would like you to know how they learned to read." Over the course of these "nightly negotiations," she asked for "that story one more time." Not just once, but over and over again!

One evening, the pleading included a glass of water. "One of my loving sisters," she said, omitting the name of the not-so-innocent, "handed me a glass filled with bubbling Alka-Seltzer." This was to make it clear that there would be no more requests that evening. Kim gave no further details on the outcome of the Alka-Seltzer, leaving it to our imaginations, and summed up the story, saying that "having a five-year-old in the house" had given her a new perspective on bedtime routines.

Sidekicks

Of all the families we socialized with when we were growing up, we spent the most time with Ken and Eleanore and their family. We ate many a Sunday dinner at their home, and they at ours. We went on long drives together in summer, taking along a picnic lunch, and in winter, we skated on frozen ponds in the fields. Later, when there were enough of us to make a team, we played baseball together in their yard or ours.

On the same Sunday in August every summer, we went to Ipperwash beach together. Mom made a picnic lunch, and we'd gather swimsuits and towels, beach ball, and pails and shovels from our sandbox.

When Ken and Eleanore drove in the lane with their Volkswagen van, we knew it was just about time to leave.

"Can we ride with them?" we'd ask. Riding in their van always made the drive to the lake seem shorter.

When we arrived at Ipperwash, it was about lunch time, but we'd run in the water for a quick splash while our mothers got lunch unpacked.

We built sandcastles on the beach, and half buried Ken in the sand so that only his face and his feet were sticking out. Eventually, we had to set him free though. Once he made a mermaid in the sand that I wanted to take home, though I wasn't sure how that would work.

We played ball in the water with the boys, and Dad and Ken played catch with us; they seemed to have as much fun as we did. Mom and Eleanore spent most of their time on the beach with the two youngest, Joan and Marilyn, who could play only in the shallows and in the sand nearby. At the end of the day, we'd have had enough sun, the sand castles would have dried up and been whittled away by the incoming tide, and the mermaid would be looking much less like herself.

We tracked home much sand in our clothes and beach towels, along with the memories, and eventually took our moveable feast to Bayfield, when Ken and Eleanore built a cottage there.

#

I was in Grade 11 when the elementary school that my younger sisters attended offered a trip to Montreal for Expo '67. My sisters wanted to go on the trip and were allowed.

"May I go too?" My parents were agreeable to this idea and wrote a letter to my school asking permission for me to take a few days off. It was granted.

With Ken and Eleanore as our chaperones, we travelled by train, stayed in St. Jean de Brébeuf boarding school, took a bus tour of Montreal, including a look inside the Notre Dame Cathedral. Expo itself, with its crowds of people, represented so many cultures of the world and so much information that it was almost overwhelming at times. Most of us had never been outside our community, much less Ontario. We returned, tired and excited, and in time for me to write my final exams.

We had spent so much time together with Ken and Eleanore and their family during our childhood and adolescent years that it was quite a shock when they gave us the news.

"We've decided to move north."

Their announcement met with initial silence.

"We've bought a farm up there."

More silence.

They would put their farm up for sale within a week, but they wanted us and their families to know first.

It was a major decision to move so far from where they had grown up, and away from the only home their children had known, but one son's health took precedence. He would feel so much better where the air was drier and the growing season was shorter.

"How will we live without them?" we wondered. The leaving would be hard for everyone.

Our community had a special send off for them, and there were many tears the day we said our goodbyes. It was like tearing flesh from flesh. Every one of us knew the visits would be few and far between, especially when the best travelling weather coincided with our harvest.

I was married before I saw their new home in the north, eleven hours of driving time away from our home, but only a slight detour on our way home from the West.

At the time of this writing, I had recently spoken with Eleanore about our trips to Ipperwash back so many years, inquiring about photos for my parents' 60th wedding anniversary book.

"I do have a few photos, if that would help," Eleanore offered.

We agreed on a plan and her son sent those photos by email.

We still treasure the friendship and keep in touch through Christmas letters and cards, occasional phone calls, and when they come for a visit. We are always glad to see them and hope they will be able to come again.

His Own Way

I'd have to call Great Uncle Edward eccentric. I remember him sitting in the workshop with a visor on his head, the kind you might have seen on a post office employee, long before the plastic visor became popular. He made his own visors with cardboard and a piece of string. Mom says that he was probably used to wearing a headset when he worked at the telephone switching station and likely felt bare without it.

After the switching station closed, Uncle Edward moved in with his brother Bill and sister-in-law Ardena and their family and lived with them for many years.

Victims of polio at the ages of 18 and 16, brothers Bill and Edward had something in common besides being brothers, though my grandfather was left with a limp, while Edward was more seriously affected. His shoulders were slightly hunched and his back somewhat crooked. He got about short distances with a cane and crutch, especially in the house and up and down stairs. He used a wheelchair more in later years, when he had a farther distance to travel.

Edward never let his disability be a thorn in his life or anyone else's. He was independent in spirit, poked fun and teased us for silly things we did or said.

Though he was my great uncle, we all called him Uncle Edward. He had bushy eyebrows and thick dark straight hair that he wore quite long. He wore glasses only for reading, smiled often, and had a familiar chuckle when he laughed. In spite of his obvious disability, he drove a car. His car was about the same size as Grandpa's Studebaker, and its side driver's door opened to the front so he could swing his crippled leg out first. The two cars in Grandpa's garage took up a good deal of space.

#

When my grandparents moved off the farm, Great Uncle Edward moved with them, but as my Grandpa Bill started requiring more care, and my grandmother had less energy, Uncle Edward moved to one of the nursing homes in town. It was not an easy decision for them.

Even in the nursing home, he wore the visor as he read.

As he did at the farm and at the house in town, Uncle Edward often had a newspaper or magazine in hand. He kept up with the news and conversed with the staff and visitors, but time still dragged. His mind was sharp and inquisitive, and he missed the family visits he'd become accustomed to at my grandparents' home.

#

I started working at the nursing home soon after Uncle Edward moved there. As I walked the hall to attend to other residents, I listened for Uncle Edward's familiar chuckle, his "heh, heh," and I stopped and talked with him whenever I had a spare moment. If I could, I'd bring him his meal tray.

#

No matter what life had dealt him—disability from an illness no one could prevent at the time, or the need to move to the nursing home—he made the best of his situation without bitterness or a bad attitude. He was cheerful and often put a smile on our faces with his quick wit and friendly demeanor. After a visit with him, I went back to work with a smile on my face too.

Bringing the Cows Home

When I entered the small room in the nursing home, Grandpa Bill was sitting in his chair, a blue hospital gown over his pajamas, and his thinning short gray hair standing straight up, like it hadn't seen a comb that day.

"Hello," I said. "How are you feeling today?"

He stared at me through wire-rimmed glasses that sat awkwardly on his face.

"I'm going to fetch the cows from the field," he said. He grabbed hold of the bed rail and pulled it back and forth.

This was not the way I remembered him from my childhood. This was not the retired grandfather who sat in his easy chair in the evening, smoking his pipe, sometimes falling asleep, nor the loving grandpa who smiled at us when we came in the door, then tickled and teased us until we were silly, just before we had to go home to bed.

As a child, I remember seeing him heading for the field, his cap pulled low over his head, to bring the cows in for milking. He walked with a limp even then.

He and my grandmother had eight children. Grandpa took care of his herd of dairy cattle, and he grew grain and corn to feed the animals. During the Depression, Grandpa took up butchering and rented a market stand each week. Along with Grandma's home-baked pies, and their garden produce, they managed to take care of their family's needs even though cash was in limited supply.

Now Grandpa couldn't walk more than a few steps each day.

Nurse's aides helped him from his bed to the chair and back again, and his days were full of boring sameness, or so I thought.

But I was wrong about the sameness, though the room looked dull and uninteresting to me. Grandpa was reliving his earlier days. It was milking time again, and he was totally engrossed in the task he had done for so many years. His mind wasn't in his body, here in this colourless room that held a bed, a nightstand and a chair. It was in the field, in sunshine, as he brought the cows home one more time.

Memory of a Life

I wondered if the casket would be open after such a devastating illness, but it is. Breathtaking fragrance of gladioli and lilies greet us at the door, covering the delicate scent of roses and the earthy smell of baby's breath. Bouquets surround my eighty-year-old aunt, laid out in one of her Sunday dresses.

Many thoughts run through my head. It's hardly a week ago that my daughter and I participated in our first palliative care experience at her bedside. There's a lifetime of memories, too many to review on this day. My aunt has been part of my life since I was born. Indeed, she babysat me after my sister announced her imminent arrival with early birth pains. Aunt Doris, baptized Doris Caroline, shares a name with me and, late in her life, a desire to record and explore using the written word. We have shared life; she has touched many lives for good.

Once Upon a Sandbox

Here lies a woman who holds no Nobel Prize, but she worked to promote peace within her family, humanity fully intact and imperfect as we all are. There are no credits as originator of a soup kitchen for the poor and displaced, yet her home was a place for fun, laughter and good food, where guests were welcomed and school teachers provided board. Neither has she earned a medal for bravery, though her last months are a testimony to her courage in adversity, maintaining her faith in God and a questioning heart.

#

Her arms are as thin as the bones that grew with her from childhood through her adult life. Spectacles bridge her nose, tucked in place behind her ears. Aunt Doris' mouth is pursed unnaturally, as though the last sound past her lips was a whimper.

My sister, Mary, had washed and styled her godmother's short silver hair one last time, brushed it back off her face and curled at the temples in her usual style. Someone had added a touch of blush on her cheeks to push back some of the gray pallor of death.

Murmuring voices are broken by peals of laughter, over a humorous memory, no doubt, providing relief in this suppressed atmosphere. For an articulate and verbal family, this is quiet. We laugh and cry together.

As we acknowledge that my aunt's suffering is over, we also grieve the loss of a person who has meant a great deal to us. She was known as "Auntie Dodo," a name she probably invented when a young niece or nephew couldn't say her name. I remember her outstretched arms, waiting for a hug. We've shared many of those.

Doris had laughed and talked with the young members of the extended family, from the toddlers to the college bound. My youngest daughter, her great niece, remembers the shuffle board games, checkers, and homemade cookies at the Village Manor.

During her stay at the nursing home, the Women's Institute members gave her a quiet celebration on her 80th birthday and bestowed her with a lifetime service pin. Fellow volunteers of the palliative care organization visited her too, showing their respect and love.

In spite of her pain and sleepless nights, she appreciated visits, especially from her family. Always interested in my writing, published and otherwise, she saved copies for quiet reading times. We had talked about the interests we shared.

Past occasions come to mind when Aunt Doris' wit, intelligence, and decisiveness put any notions out of our heads about whether or not she was in charge of her life, insofar as humans have control. Even during her illness, as her sons contemplated the task of emptying her apartment, she was still in control. She would do it as she was able, and she did so gracefully, with the support of her family.

Visitors file by, expressing their condolences, sharing their own grief. My aunt was known by many, as her memorial cards attest. From her neighbours on the farm to those in town, members of her church family, fellow palliative care workers, and staff from the nursing home where she once worked as well as the one where she spent her last days.

One of the most touching moments was the lineup of nursing home staff, each waiting a turn to extend sympathy.

"We'll miss her."

"She was a great lady."

"We were privileged to know her."

It seems that everyone who worked there, from floor cleaners and kitchen staff to nurses, was touched by her life, her courage, and her humour. I've been blessed too.

From a Cocoon

silence descends
when someone speaks your name

cocoon silence
where no one sees   except God

not all are silent
loved ones
who shared the pain   cried
as they watched it destroy you
like a caterpillar   at the mercy of a hawk

I saw you   shut away
in iron-clad secrecy
where truth is acknowledged   in silence
where doors meant to protect you
cocooned you away from loved ones
and well-meaning souls tried to
rescue what was left

God knew your pain

The sealed cocoon   so tightly guarded
has broken open   a butterfly
has spread its wings and flown beyond our reach

now God holds you to himself
and wipes away your tears
and we wait to see you smiling once again

One Last Moonlight

A vacant house
dim as moonlight's glow
in its west windows
bare of brocade and lace

once a proud house
shelter from the heat and cold
rain and snow
hosting games of hide and seek
laughter and song
Sunday family dinner
its doorpost etched with children's growth
a notch for every measure
wooden stairs worn smooth
by a hundred pairs of feet
tearful good-byes at the front door

thistle and wild carrot grow
where civilized gardens flourished
a leaning picket fence weathered down to its
wood

it's a sad house
naked before the wrecking ball
sagging roof and weeping foundation
peeling paint and chipping plaster

tonight
the man in the moon
gazes lovingly upon the house
that tomorrow will render to
memory

February Grief

February's white storm wraps my family into itself
with chain-studded tires
and hope that the storm will break

Grandmother's bond with this wintry earth
has come untied
my mind photographs
a pall-draped coffin
grief envelops me   alone
trembling fingers on ivory keys
my mind singing the words
my throat holds back

I miss her

Goodbye to the Old Farm House

Years after Mom's parents, as well as some of her siblings, had died, one of her sisters received a call from the owners of their home farm. The family had built a new house on the property and the old one would soon be taken down. Would they care to go through the house one last time?

What an unexpected but delightful surprise!

Mom and two of her sisters made an appointment with the family to tour the house and recall their childhood memories in that place. I can imagine the walk through being both happy and sad. Happy to recall good memories there, and sad to see its end with so few of them left.

When Mom told me about the house tour sometime later, I, too, thought back to my visits there, but only in my memory, for the house was long gone by then. A grassy patch now covered the place where the house once stood. I had memories too—certainly not as many as my mother, but my mind played on a scene of the house on its last night, and I thought of how the moon would shine on it and of the memories that the house would share if only it could speak.

Conclusion

Living on a farm, one marks seasons by the cycle of planting and harvest. In winter, when the earth is at rest, its caretakers are free to engage in other pursuits. Farm owners celebrate periods of plenty, always dependent on the right weather—enough rainfall, sufficient sun—not to mention the energy to get all the work done. There are also periods of low yields and high prices that are beyond their control.

What one takes from the soil must be replenished in some way. One cannot take and take and expect the earth to keep on producing, and so a wise manager feeds the soil, rotates crops, and allows years of fallow for the soil to regenerate. Farm owners are stewards of the land, of creation. They have also been the first recyclers.

Farm management comes with close attention to costs and benefits, and frugal and reasoned spending. I learned to accept, even when it was difficult, that purchases depended on the price of eggs or the price of stock being sold at market. If the price was up, we spent dollars on the new garage or the roller skates. If it was down, we still got what we needed, but maybe not as much of it. Through my parents' thrifty example, I learned how to use my income wisely and save some for a "rainy day," to share with others from my abundance, to trust God, and to manage with what I have when work is slow.

As in any field of endeavour, farm owners who want to do well and keep on farming learn best practices for crops and their dairy herds, pigs or chickens. They also give constant attention to the upkeep of their buildings.

Farm owners take care of their own health as well as the health and education of their children. They take time for recreation and play. Many still value their day of rest and take time for worship. These families work the land to provide food for themselves, the wider community, and the cities. They make use of opportunities to learn through groups dedicated to rural living, such as the Women's Institutes, agricultural societies, 4-H clubs and through public and private educational resources.

I cannot imagine how different it might have been growing up in another place; the country was my home and my way of being. I had room to run in the great outdoors with my siblings, friends and cousins. I was clothed and fed, educated and loved. I walked or rode the bus to school and returned home at the end of that school day to help with tasks that were waiting to be done.

My parents gave us the opportunity for music lessons, high school and post-secondary education and gave their blessings on the career paths we chose to follow. While their formal education stopped the day they left grade school, they continued to learn and use their God-given gifts in whatever they did. My parents, like their parents before them, knew the importance of thrift and managed their farms well through poor crops and prices, and in plenty.

I've been blessed by my relationships with our wider family, grandparents, aunts, uncles and cousins, friends and neighbours, many of whom are kindred spirits and a part of my life today.

They, too, taught lessons of compassion, hard work and endurance, sometimes against difficult challenges.

I have benefitted from many teachers, both in my formal education, in the one-room school house and beyond, as well as from people outside the classroom who would not necessarily call themselves teachers, women who taught our 4-H club units, those who made 4-H possible, piano and choir teachers and leaders, pastors, interns, and teachers of my Sunday school classes, all of whom imparted some insight or knowledge, whether or not they realized it.

As I close this work, I ponder anew the mysteries of creation, how the sun and rain make crops grow, crops that start as tiny seeds, the mysterious unfolding already written into their cells. The process that makes corn seeds develop into plants that feed many, that starts a seed or seedling that grows into a tree or bush and produces food to feed our bodies, all of it begun by the one who created humankind and provided for our needs. It is an awesome and wonderful thing.

Writing Your Own Stories

You want to write? Good, then it's time to get started.

If the thought of writing a whole book is overwhelming, start by writing one personal essay. Set it aside for a while, a week or two, and go on to another piece. Go back to your first story; polish it and revise it. Do this with each piece you write. Writers revise many times, and you need to do this too.

If you're serious about writing, get a collegiate dictionary, a thesaurus and a grammar book or two. Finally, look up a writer's group in your area. By being part of such a group, you get feedback on your material while you help others polish their writing.

Resources that may be helpful for digging up memories and writing the stories:
- *Writing personal essays: How to shape your life experiences for the page*, by Sheila Bender, 1995, Writer's Digest Books
- *You Can Write a Memoir*, by Susan Carol Hauser, 2001, Writer's Digest Books
- *Writing life stories: how to make memories into memoirs, ideas into essays, and life into literature*, by Bill Roorbach with Kristen Keckler, 2008, Writer's Digest Books
- *Using Stories and Humour: Grab Your Audience*, by Joanna Slan, 1998, Allyn & Bacon
- *You don't have to be famous: How to write your life story*, author Steve Zousmer, 2007, Writer's Digest Books

About the Author

C. R. Wilker grew up in rural Oxford County. Her career has been varied, beginning as an early childhood educator, to making and selling craft items, operating a small sewing business, and later writing and editing, speaking and storytelling.

Publishing credits include articles, op-eds, inspirational and devotional pieces, book reviews, poetry, and creative non-fiction in regional to international publications.

She is an award-winning poet with credits in *Tower Poetry; Esprit; Glad Tidings; Tickled by Thunder; Writers Undercover, vol. x; Voices and Visions, vol. 6; Favourite Poems Contest Anthology* by Craigleigh Press. Her poem "Waiting Room" tied for third in the Inscribe Christian Writer's Fall contest in 2008 and has since been published in *Grounded,* a chapbook of her published poetry.

Also in 2008, her creative non-fiction piece "Anticipated Visits" was published in *The Wisdom of Old Souls*. Another poem "Sails on a Quilted Sea" was published in an anthology called *Grandmothers' Necklace*, a fund-raiser for the Stephen Lewis Foundation.

Previously Published Pieces

"Pencils, Lunchboxes and Compositions" from The Waterloo Region Record, 2004, revised and retitled.

"Bush Walk" in Writers Undercover, Vol. X, 2004.

Poems "Once Upon a Sandbox", "Frozen Weeds Were Goalposts", "One Last Moonlight", "Kitchen Talk", "Bush Walk" and "A Nickel to Spend" published by Tower Poetry, 2004-2009.

"Just Like Daddy" in Esprit, 2006.

"Anticipated Visits" in The Wisdom of Old Souls, by Hidden Brook Press, 2008.

Bibliography

Bender, Sheila. *Writing personal essays: How to shape your life experiences for the page*. Cincinnati, Ohio: Writer's Digest Books, 1995.

Federated Women's Institutes of Ontario. "Advocacy Update." *Home and Country*, Spring/Summer 2009, p. 11.

Federated Women's Institutes of Ontario. *Ontario Women's Institute Story*. 1972.

Federated Women's Institutes of Ontario: Accessed July 25, 2009. http://www.fwio.on.ca/Contribute/advocacy/PastResolutions.

Hauser, Susan Carol. *You Can Write a Memoir*. Cincinnati, Ohio: Writer's Digest Books, 2001.

Oxford North District Women's Institute. *Our Anniversary Album of Memories*. 1980.

Oxford North Women's Institute. *Fiftieth Anniversary: 1905-1955*, 1955.

Roorbach, Bill, and Kristen Keckler, PhD. *Writing Life Stories: How to Make Memories into Memoirs, Ideas into Essays, and Life into Literature*. Cincinnati, Ohio: Writer's Digest Books, 2008.

Seltzer, Karl, ed. *Fact and Fantasy: A History of Tavistock*. Rotary Club of Tavistock, 1967.

Slan, Joanna. *Using Stories and Humour: Grab Your Audience*. Needham Heights, MA: Allyn & Bacon, 1998.

Zousmer, Steve. *You Don't Have to Be Famous: How to Write Your Life Story*. Cincinnati, Ohio: Writer's Digest Books, 2007.

4-H Ontario. Accessed July 31, 2009. http://www.4-hontario.ca/county.aspx?countyid=69

[1] See "Good Cooks."
[2] See "Entertainment."
[3] See "Trip to the Woodlot."
[4] See "Federated Women's Institutes and 4-H Girls' Clubs."
[5] See "Farm Pets."
[6] See "Farm Pets."
[7] See "What a Car!"
[8] See "Anticipated Visits."
[9] See "One Last Moonlight."
[10] See "His Own Way."
[11] See "Crochet Lessons."
[12] Karl Seltzer, ed., *Fact and Fantasy* (Tavistock: Rotary Club, 1967), 107.
[13] Federated Women's Institutes of Ontario, *Ontario Women's Institute Story*, 6.
[14] 4-H is a club for young people growing up in the country. The four Hs stand for Head, Heart, Hands and Health and are part of a pledge we repeated at each meeting.
[15] See "Garden Club."
[16] Federated Women's Institutes of Ontario, "Advocacy Update." *Home & Country Rose Garden*, Spring and Summer (2009):11.
[17] See "Granny Square."
[18] 4-H is a club for young people growing up in the country. The four Hs stand for Head, Heart, Hands and Health and are part of a pledge we repeated at each meeting.
[19] 4-H Pledge: I pledge my head to clearer thinking, my heart to greater loyalty, my hands to larger service, and my health to better living for my club, my community and my country.